LERMONTOV'S NOVICE
(МЦЫРИ)

LERMONTOV'S NOVICE

(МЦЫРИ)

RUSSIAN TEXT, ACCENTED

WITH INTRODUCTION, NOTES, AND VOCABULARY

BY

J. D. DUFF, M.A.

FELLOW OF TRINITY COLLEGE

CAMBRIDGE

AT THE UNIVERSITY PRESS

1919

CAMBRIDGE
UNIVERSITY PRESS

University Printing House, Cambridge CB2 8BS, United Kingdom

Published in the United States of America by Cambridge University Press, New York

Cambridge University Press is part of the University of Cambridge.

It furthers the University's mission by disseminating knowledge in the pursuit of education, learning and research at the highest international levels of excellence.

www.cambridge.org
Information on this title: www.cambridge.org/9781107676848

© Cambridge University Press 1919

First published 1919
First paperback edition 2014

A catalogue record for this publication is available from the British Library

ISBN 978-1-107-67684-8 Paperback

PREFACE

THIS text of Lérmontov's poem has been printed from the seventh edition of his works, published at Petersburg in 1889. The accents have been added here and throughout the book.

The Notes are intended to explain briefly whatever seemed likely to puzzle a reader fairly familiar with the elements of Russian accidence. Points of importance have been purposely stated more than once, and there are many references from one passage in the text or notes to another.

An Appendix contains a summary account, reprinted from my *Russian Lyrics*, of the perfective and imperfective aspects of the verb. I believe it will prove useful to beginners; but they must realise that it is only a summary account of a large and difficult subject.

The Vocabulary contains all the words which occur in the text; and many words are entered under more than one heading. In compiling the Vocabulary I was much helped by P. W. Duff, Scholar of Winchester College.

My chief obligations are to Mr Nevill Forbes's *Russian Grammar* (Oxford 1914), Garbell's *Das russische Zeitwort* (Berlin 1901), Dal's *Dictionary* (1903), and Boyer and Speranski's *Russian Reader* (Chicago edition).

J. D. DUFF.

November 11, 1918.

CONTENTS

INTRODUCTION

I.

MICHAEL LÉRMONTOV was born at Moscow on October 2nd, 1814; he was killed in a duel on July 15th, 1841, before he had completed his twenty-seventh year. Not five years had passed since Púshkin, the greatest of Russian poets and men of letters, lost his life in the same way at the age of thirty-eight.

Of the details of Lérmontov's short life not much is known. He traced his descent from the Scottish family of Learmonth, and sometimes expresses in his poetry a wish to visit the land of his ancestors, of which he perhaps derived his ideas chiefly from Ossian. He might possibly have been a visitor at Abbotsford, where his surname alone would have been a passport to Scott's favour; for Learmonth is the name assigned by local tradition and ancient authorities to Thomas the Rymer, a personage in whom Scott took a deep interest. He lost his mother before he was three, and was brought up by his grandmother, chiefly at Moscow. After studying for some time at Moscow University, then the central point of Russian education and intelligence, he entered the Army and saw some active service in the Caucasus, where he had been sent as a punishment for the sentiments expressed in his poetry, and especially for the verses he had written on the death of Púshkin.

It was at a watering-place in the Caucasus that the fatal duel took place. The origin of the quarrel has never been satisfactorily explained; his antagonist, a Major Martýnov, lived till 1876, and he was more than once invited to publish a statement of the circumstances; but he refused, and the mystery will never be solved. That Lérmontov was difficult to live with, is likely enough: he was conscious of great powers and had found little peace or happiness in life.

II.

The piety of Russian editors is perhaps excessive, and a good deal of what Lérmontov wrote might with advantage have been suppressed. Thus *Ismail Bey*, the longest of his poems, is feeble both in plan and execution; it was an early work, written in 1832. He developed his powers slowly, and his best work, which gives him his high and secure place among Russian writers, was done in the last years of his short life.

He left a novel, or succession of scenes, in prose, *A Hero of Our Time*, a number of admirable lyrics, and three longer poems—*The Merchant Kaláshnikov*, *The Demon*, and *Mtsýri*, or *The Novice*. The first of these is perhaps his masterpiece—an epic ballad with real Homeric quality; and it is remarkable as the only one of his longer poems in which Lérmontov is not drawing a picture of himself. In general, one must say of him that he was too exclusively occupied with "the pageant of his bleeding heart." It was a gorgeous pageant as he painted it; but it palls at last upon the reader. The *Demon* is a lay-figure, invented to express Lérmontov's own feelings; and *Mtsýri* is another.

III.

On May 9th, 1840, Gógol kept his thirty-first birthday at Moscow. Pogódin, a prominent figure in literary circles, entertained him at a dinner in his garden; and Gógol, who enjoyed this operation as heartily as Mr Micawber, made punch for the party afterwards. We are told that Turgénev was present; and it is remarkable that he makes no mention of the occasion in his scanty recollections of Lérmontov. Lérmontov, however, was there, and read parts of his new poem, *Mtsýri*, to the assembled company. It was published in 1840; and from that day to this the poem has been a prime

favourite with the Russian people, and their foremost critics
have justified the general opinion; there was no verse (we
learn from Turgénev) which Byelínski recited with more
pleasure or with more effect. It is, indeed, a masterpiece of its
kind, strong and brilliant from the first line to the last. The
tone of the speaker is unpleasing, in its hard self-satisfaction;
but that belongs to the character. Nor is it probable that a
man so near death should be capable of such a prodigious
volubility; but the reader pardons the improbability for the
sake of the poem.

IV.

The metre calls for some notice, because it is exceptional
in Russian literature. The metrical scheme itself is common,
and was used by both Púshkin and Lérmontov in all their
longer poems; in English it is less familiar; and our chief
examples of it are to be found in Butler's *Hudibras* and
Swift's verse. Each line consists of four iambic feet, like this
line from Coleridge's *Christabel*—

> They párted—né'er to meét agaín.

But Lérmontov in this poem makes two striking departures
from the usual practice.

First, he has not a single instance of a double rhyme,
such as

> The bránds were flát, the bránds were *dýing*,
> Amíd their ówn white áshes *lýing*,

though these occur constantly in other Russian poems, written
by himself and others in this metre. In *Mtsýri*, the final
stress in every line falls on the last syllable. And, secondly,
the rhyme is never delayed, so as to weave the verse into
stanzas: the second line rhymes to the first, the fourth to the
third, and so on to the end of the poem. This is quite
exceptional.

Russians often complain that our monosyllabic rhymes are
monotonous to their ear; and Lérmontov devised a plan to

secure some variety. His plan is to write, at uncertain intervals, three or even four consecutive lines, with the same rhyme: the entire poem contains 748 verses, and this device is repeated fifty-four times.

The reader should notice how much stricter Russian metrical practice is than our own. Neither trochee ($-\cup$) or spondee ($--$) is allowed: every foot in the verse is a real iambus, with the accent on the second syllable; and, further, an anapaest ($\cup\cup-$) is never admitted as equivalent to an iambus ($\cup-$). Such a line as Coleridge's

Save the bóss of the shiéld of Sir Léoline táll

will be sought in vain in Lérmontov or Púshkin, when they are writing iambic verse. Much of the verse written by Coleridge, Scott, and Byron resembles that of *Mtsýri* in this respect, that each line has four stresses; but our poets allow themselves much greater freedom in their metre.

МЦЫРИ.

Вкуша́я вкуси́хъ ма́ло мёда, и се
азъ умира́ю.
       I Кни́га Ца́рствъ.

I.

Не мно́го лѣтъ тому́ наза́дъ,
Тамъ, гдѣ слива́яся шумя́тъ,
Обня́вшись, бу́дто двѣ сестры́,
Струи́ Ара́гвы и Куры́,
Былъ монасты́рь. Изъ-за горы́   5
И ны́нче ви́дитъ пѣшехо́дъ
Столбы́ обру́шенныхъ воро́тъ,
И ба́шни, и церко́вный сво́дъ;
Но не кури́тся ужъ подъ нимъ
Кади́льницъ благово́нный дымъ,   10
Не слы́шно пѣнья въ по́здній часъ
Моля́щихъ и́ноковъ за насъ.
Тепе́рь оди́нъ стари́къ сѣдо́й,
Разва́линъ стражъ полуживо́й,
Людьми́ и сме́ртію забы́тъ,   15
Смета́етъ пыль съ моги́льныхъ плитъ,
Кото́рыхъ на́дпись говори́тъ
О сла́вѣ про́шлой—и о томъ,
Какъ, удручёнъ свои́мъ вѣнцо́мъ,
Тако́й-то царь, въ тако́й-то годъ,   20
Вручи́лъ Росси́и свой наро́дъ.

*

И Божья благодать сошла
На Грузію!—Она цвѣла
Съ тѣхъ поръ въ тѣни своихъ садовъ,
Не опасаяся враговъ,   25
За гранью дружескихъ штыковъ.

II.

Однажды русскій генералъ
Изъ горъ къ Тифлису проѣзжалъ;
Ребёнка плѣннаго онъ вёзъ.
Тотъ занемогъ, не перенёсъ   30
Трудовъ далёкаго пути.
Онъ былъ, казалось, лѣтъ шести;
Какъ серна горъ, пугливъ и дикъ,
И слабъ и гибокъ, какъ тростникъ;
Но въ нёмъ мучительный недугъ   35
Развилъ тогда могучій духъ
Его отцовъ. Безъ жалобъ онъ
Томился, даже слабый стонъ
Изъ дѣтскихъ губъ не вылеталъ,
Онъ знакомъ пищу отвергалъ,   40
И тихо, гордо умиралъ.
Изъ жалости одинъ монахъ
Больнаго призрѣлъ, и въ стѣнахъ
Хранительныхъ остался онъ,
Искусствомъ дружескимъ спасёнъ.   45
Но, чуждъ ребяческихъ утѣхъ,
Сначала бѣгалъ онъ отъ всѣхъ,
Бродилъ безмолвенъ, одинокъ,
Смотрѣлъ вздыхая на востокъ,
Томимъ неясною тоской   50

По сторонѣ своей роднóй.
Но послѣ къ плѣну онъ привы́къ,
Сталъ понимáть чужóй язы́къ,
Былъ окрещёнъ святы́мъ отцóмъ
И, съ шýмнымъ свѣтомъ незнакóмъ,   55
Ужé хотѣлъ во цвѣтѣ лѣтъ
Изрéчь монáшескій обѣтъ,
Какъ вдругъ однáжды онъ исчéзъ
Осéнней нóчью. Тёмный лѣсъ
Тянýлся по горáмъ кругóмъ.   60
Три дня всѣ пóиски по нёмъ
Напрáсны бы́ли ; но потóмъ
Егó въ степи́ безъ чувствъ нашли́
И вновь въ обѝтель принесли́.
Онъ стрáшно блѣденъ былъ и худъ   65
И слабъ, какъ бýдто дóлгій трудъ,
Болѣзнь, иль гóлодъ испытáлъ.
Онъ на допрóсъ не отвѣчáлъ
И съ кáждымъ днёмъ примѣтно вялъ.
И блѝзокъ сталъ его конéцъ.   70
Тогдá пришёлъ къ немý чернéцъ
Съ увѣщевáньемъ и мольбóй ;
И, гóрдо вы́слушавъ, больнóй
Привстáлъ, собрáвъ остáтокъ силъ,
И дóлго такъ онъ говори́лъ :   75

III.

«Ты слýшать ѝсповѣдь мою
Сюдá пришёлъ, благодарю́.
Всё лýчше пéредъ кѣмъ-нибýдь
Словáми облегчи́ть мнѣ грудь ;

Но лю́дямъ я не дѣ́лалъ зла,   80
И потому́ мои́ дѣла́
Не мно́го по́льзы вамъ узна́ть—
А ду́шу мо́жно ль разсказа́ть?
Я ма́ло жилъ, и жилъ въ плѣну́.
Таки́хъ двѣ жи́зни за одну́,   85
Но то́лько по́лную трево́гъ,
Я промѣня́лъ бы, е́сли бъ могъ.
Я зналъ одно́й лишь ду́мы власть,
Одну́ но пла́менную страсть:
Она́ какъ червь во мнѣ жила́,   90
Изгры́зла ду́шу и сожгла́.
Она́ мечты́ мои́ звала́
Отъ ке́лій ду́шныхъ и моли́твъ
Въ тотъ чу́дный міръ трево́гъ и битвъ,
Гдѣ въ ту́чахъ пря́чутся скалы́,   95
Гдѣ лю́ди во́льны, какъ орлы́.
Я э́ту страсть во тьмѣ ночно́й
Вскорми́лъ слеза́ми и тоско́й;
Её предъ не́бомъ и землёй
Я ны́нѣ гро́мко признаю́   100
И о проще́ньи не молю́.

IV.

«Стари́къ! я слы́шалъ мно́го разъ,
Что ты меня́ отъ сме́рти спа́съ.
Заче́мъ?... Угрю́мъ и одино́къ,
Грозо́й ото́рванный листо́къ,   105
Я вы́росъ въ су́мрачныхъ стѣна́хъ,
Душо́й дитя́, судьбо́й мона́хъ.
Я никому́ не могъ сказа́ть

Свяще́нныхъ словъ «оте́цъ» и «мать».
Коне́чно, ты хотѣ́лъ, стари́къ,   110
Чтобъ я въ оби́тели отвы́къ
Отъ э́тихъ сла́достныхъ име́нъ—
Напра́сно: звукъ ихъ былъ рождёнъ
Со мной. Я ви́дѣлъ у други́хъ
Отчи́зну, домъ, друзе́й, родны́хъ,   115
А у себя́ не находи́лъ
Не то́лько ми́лыхъ душъ—моги́лъ!
То́гда, пусты́хъ не тра́тя слёзъ,
Въ душѣ́ я кля́тву произнёсъ:
Хотя́ на мигъ, когда́ нибу́дь,   120
Мою́ пыла́ющую грудь
Прижа́ть съ тоско́й къ груди́ друго́й,
Хоть незнако́мой, но родно́й.
Увы́! тепе́рь мечта́нья тѣ
Поги́бли въ по́лной красотѣ́,   125
И я, какъ жилъ, въ землѣ́ чужо́й
Умру́ рабо́мъ и сирото́й.

V.

«Меня́ моги́ла не страши́тъ:
Тамъ, говоря́тъ, страда́нье спитъ
Въ холо́дной вѣ́чной тишинѣ́.   130
Но съ жи́знью жаль разста́ться мнѣ́.
Я мо́лодъ, мо́лодъ... зналъ ли ты
Разгу́льной ю́ности мечты́,
Или́ не зналъ? или́ забы́лъ,
Какъ ненави́дѣлъ и люби́лъ?   135
Какъ се́рдце би́лося живѣ́й
При ви́дѣ со́лнца и поле́й

Съ высо́кой ба́шни угловой,
Гдѣ во́здухъ свѣжъ, и гдѣ поро́й
Въ глубо́кой сква́жинѣ стѣны́,
Дитя́ невѣ́домой страны́,
Прижа́вшись, го́лубь молодо́й
Сиди́тъ, испу́ганный грозо́й?
Пуска́й тепе́рь прекра́сный свѣтъ
Тебѣ́ посты́лъ: ты слабъ, ты сѣдъ,
И отъ жела́ній ты отвы́къ.
Что за нужда́? Ты жилъ, стари́къ!
Тебѣ́ есть въ мі́рѣ что́ забы́ть,
Ты жилъ—я та́кже могъ бы жить!

VI.

«Ты хо́чешь знать, что ви́дѣлъ я
На во́лѣ?—Пы́шныя поля́,
Холмы́, покры́тые вѣнцо́мъ
Дере́въ, разро́сшихся круго́мъ,
Шумя́щихъ свѣ́жею толпо́й,
Какъ бра́тья въ пля́скѣ круговой.
Я ви́дѣлъ гру́ды тёмныхъ скалъ,
Когда́ пото́къ ихъ раздѣля́лъ,
И ду́мы ихъ я угада́лъ:
Мнѣ бы́ло свы́ше то́ дано́!
Простёрты въ во́здухѣ давно́,
Объя́тья ка́менныя ихъ
И жа́ждутъ встрѣ́чи ка́ждый мигъ;
Но дни бѣгу́тъ, бѣгу́тъ года́—
Имъ не сойти́ться никогда́!
Я ви́дѣлъ го́рные хребты́,
Причу́дливые какъ мечты́,

140

145

150

155

160

165

Когда́ въ часъ у́тренней зари́
Кури́лися какъ алтари́
Ихъ вы́си въ не́бѣ голубо́мъ,
И о́блачко за о́блачкомъ,   170
Поки́нувъ та́йный свой ночле́гъ,
Къ восто́ку направля́ло бѣгъ,
Какъ бу́дто бѣлый карава́нъ
Залётныхъ птицъ изъ ра́зныхъ странъ!
Вдали́ я ви́дѣлъ сквозь тума́нъ,   175
Въ снѣга́хъ, горя́щихъ какъ алма́зъ,
Сѣдо́й, незы́блемый Кавка́зъ—
И бы́ло се́рдцу моему́
Легко́, не зна́ю почему́.
Мнѣ та́йный го́лосъ говори́лъ,   180
Что нѣ́когда и я́ тамъ жилъ,
И ста́ло въ па́мяти мое́й
Проше́дшее яснѣ́й, яснѣ́й...

VII.

«И вспо́мнилъ я отцо́вскій домъ,
Уще́лье на́ше, и круго́мъ   185
Въ тѣ́ни разсы́панный ау́лъ;
Мнѣ слы́шался вече́рній гулъ
Домо́й бѣгу́щихъ табуно́въ
И да́льній лай знако́мыхъ псовъ.
Я по́мнилъ сму́глыхъ старико́въ,   190
При свѣ́тѣ лу́нныхъ вечеро́въ
Проти́въ отцо́вскаго крыльца́
Сидѣ́вшихъ съ ва́жностью лица́;
И блескъ опра́вленныхъ ноже́нъ
Кинжа́ловъ дли́нныхъ... и какъ сонъ   195

Всё это смутной чередой
Вдругъ пробѣжало предо мной.
А мой отецъ? Онъ какъ живой
Въ своей одеждѣ боевой
Являлся мнѣ, и помнилъ я   200
Кольчуги звонъ, и блескъ ружья,
И гордый, непреклонный взоръ;
И молодыхъ моихъ сестёръ...
Лучи ихъ сладостныхъ очей,
И звукъ ихъ пѣсенъ и рѣчей   205
Надъ колыбѣлію моей.
Въ ущельи томъ бѣжалъ потокъ,
Онъ шуменъ былъ, но неглубокъ;
Къ нему, на золотой песокъ,
Играть я въ полдень уходилъ   210
И взоромъ ласточекъ слѣдилъ,
Когда онѣ передъ дождёмъ
Волны касалися крыломъ.
И вспомнилъ я нашъ мирный домъ
И предъ вечернимъ очагомъ   215
Разсказы долгіе о томъ,
Какъ жили люди прежнихъ дней,
Когда былъ міръ ещё пышнѣй.

VIII.

«Ты хочешь знать, что дѣлалъ я
На волѣ? Жилъ—и жизнь моя   220
Безъ этихъ трёхъ блаженныхъ дней
Была бъ печальнѣй и мрачнѣй
Безсильной старости твоей.
Давнымъ-давно задумалъ я

Взглянуть на дальнія поля;   225
Узнать, прекрасна ли земля;
Узнать, для воли иль тюрьмы
На этотъ свѣтъ родимся мы—
И въ часъ ночной, ужасный часъ,
Когда гроза пугала васъ,   230
Когда, столпясь при алтарѣ,
Вы ницъ лежали на землѣ,
Я убѣжалъ. О! я какъ братъ
Обняться съ бурей былъ бы радъ,
Глазами тучи я слѣдилъ,   235
Рукою молнію ловилъ.
Скажи мнѣ, что средь этихъ стѣнъ
Могли бы дать вы мнѣ взамѣнъ
Той дружбы краткой, но живой,
Межъ бурнымъ сердцемъ и грозой?...   240

IX.

«Бѣжалъ я долго—гдѣ? куда?
Не знаю! Ни одна звѣзда
Не озаряла трудный путь.
Мнѣ было весело вдохнуть
Въ мою измученную грудь   245
Ночную свѣжесть тѣхъ лѣсовъ—
И только. Много я часовъ
Бѣжалъ, и наконецъ, уставъ,
Прилёгъ между высокихъ травъ;
Прислушался: погони нѣтъ.   250
Гроза утихла. Блѣдный свѣтъ
Тянулся длинной полосой
Межъ тёмнымъ небомъ и землёй,

И различалъ я, какъ узоръ,
На ней зубцы далёкихъ горъ.   255
Недвижимъ, молча, я лежалъ.
Порой въ ущеліи шакалъ
Кричалъ и плакалъ какъ дитя,
И, гладкой чешуёй блестя,
Змѣя скользила межъ камней;   260
Но страхъ не сжалъ души моей;
Я самъ, какъ звѣрь, былъ чуждъ людей,
И ползъ и прятался какъ змѣй.

X.

«Внизу глубоко подо мной
Потокъ, усиленный грозой,   265
Шумѣлъ, и шумъ его глухой
Сердитыхъ сотнѣ голосовъ
Подобился. Хотя безъ словъ,
Мнѣ внятенъ былъ тотъ разговоръ,
Немолчный ропотъ, вѣчный споръ   270
Съ упрямой грудою камней.
То вдругъ стихалъ онъ, то сильнѣй
Онъ раздавался въ тишинѣ;
И вотъ, въ туманной вышинѣ
Запѣли птички, и востокъ   275
Озолотился; вѣтерокъ
Сырые шевельнулъ листы;
Дохнули сонные цвѣты,
И какъ они, навстрѣчу дню
Я поднялъ голову мою...   280
Я осмотрѣлся; не таю:
Мнѣ стало страшно; на краю

Грозя́щей бе́здны я лежа́лъ,
Гдѣ вылъ, крутя́сь, серди́тый валъ;
Туда́ вели́ ступе́ни скалъ: 285
Но лишь злой духъ по нимъ шага́лъ,
Когда́, низве́рженный съ небе́съ,
Въ подзёмной про́пасти исче́зъ.

XI.

«Круго́мъ меня́ цвѣлъ Бо́жій садъ;
Расте́ній ра́дужный наря́дъ   290
Храни́лъ слѣды́ небе́сныхъ слёзъ,
И ку́дри виногра́дныхъ лозъ
Вили́сь, красу́ясь межъ дере́въ
Прозра́чной зе́ленью листо́въ;
И гро́зды по́лные на нихъ,   295
Серёгъ подо́бье дороги́хъ,
Висѣли пы́шно, и поро́й
Къ нимъ птицъ лета́лъ пугли́вый рой.
И сно́ва я къ землѣ припа́лъ,
И сно́ва вслу́шиваться сталъ   300
Къ волше́бнымъ, стра́ннымъ голоса́мъ;
Они́ шепта́лись по куста́мъ,
Какъ бу́дто рѣчь свою́ вели́
О та́йнахъ не́ба и земли́;
И всѣ приро́ды голоса́   305
Слива́лись тутъ; не раздался́
Въ торже́ственный хвале́нья часъ
Лишь человѣка го́рдый гласъ.
Всё, что̀ я чу́вствовалъ тогда́,
Тѣ ду́мы—имъ ужъ нѣтъ слѣда́—   310
Но я бъ жела́лъ ихъ разсказа́ть,

Чтобъ жить, хоть мысленно, опять.
Въ то утро былъ небесный сводъ
Такъ чистъ, что ангела полётъ
Прилежный взоръ слѣдить бы могъ;   315
Онъ такъ прозрачно былъ глубокъ,
Такъ полонъ ровной синевой!
Я въ нёмъ глазами и душой
Тонулъ, пока полдневный зной
Мои мечты не разогналъ,   320
И жаждой я томиться сталъ.

XII.

«Тогда къ потоку съ высоты,
Держась за гибкіе кусты,
Съ плиты на плиту я, какъ могъ,
Спускаться началъ. Изъ-подъ ногъ   325
Сорвавшись, камень иногда
Катился внизъ—за нимъ бразда
Дымилась, прахъ вился столбомъ;
Гудя и прыгая, потомъ
Онъ поглощаемъ былъ волной;   330
И я висѣлъ надъ глубиной—
Но юность вольная сильна,
И смерть казалась не страшна!
Лишь только я съ крутыхъ высотъ
Спустился, свѣжесть горныхъ водъ   335
Повѣяла навстрѣчу мнѣ,
И жадно я припалъ къ волнѣ.
Вдругъ голосъ—лёгкій шумъ шаговъ...
Мгновенно скрывшись межъ кустовъ,
Невольнымъ трепетомъ объятъ,   340

Я по́днялъ боязли́вый взглядъ
И жа́дно вслу́шиваться сталъ:
И бли́же, бли́же всё звуча́лъ
Грузи́нки го́лосъ молодо́й,
Такъ безъиску́сственно живо́й,   345
Такъ сла́дко во́льный, бу́дто онъ
Лишь зву́ки дру́жескихъ имёнъ
Произноси́ть былъ пріучёнъ.
Проста́я пѣсня то́ была́,
Но въ мысль она́ мнѣ залегла́,   350
И мнѣ, лишь су́мракъ настаётъ,
Незри́мый духъ её поётъ.

XIII.

«Держа́ кувши́нъ надъ голово́й,
Грузи́нка у́зкою тропо́й
Сходи́ла къ бе́регу. Поро́й   355
Она́ скользи́ла межъ камне́й,
Смѣя́сь нело́вкости свое́й.
И бѣденъ былъ ея́ наря́дъ;
И шла она́ легко́, наза́дъ
Изги́бы дли́нные чадры́   360
Отки́нувъ. Лѣ́тніе жары́
Покры́ли тѣ́нью золото́й
Лицо́ и грудь ея́; и зной
Дыша́лъ отъ устъ ея́ и щёкъ.
И мракъ оче́й былъ такъ глубо́къ,   365
Такъ по́лонъ та́йнами любви́,
Что ду́мы пы́лкія мой
Смути́лись. По́мню то́лько я
Кувши́на звонъ, когда́ струя́

Вливалась медленно въ него,   370
И шорохъ... больше ничего.
Когда же я очнулся вновь
И отлила отъ сердца кровь,
Она была ужъ далеко;
И шла хоть тише—но легко,   375
Стройна подъ ношею своей,
Какъ тополь, царь ея полей.
Недалеко въ прохладной мглѣ,
Казалось, приросли къ скалѣ
Двѣ сакли дружною четой;   380
Надъ плоской кровлею одной
Дымокъ струился голубой.
Я вижу будто бы теперь,
Какъ отперлась тихонько дверь
И затворилася опять.   385
— Тебѣ, я знаю, не понять
Мою тоску, мою печаль;
И если бъ могъ, мнѣ было бъ жаль:
Воспоминанья тѣхъ минутъ
Во мнѣ, со мной пускай умрутъ.   390

XIV.

«Трудами ночи изнурёнъ,
Я лёгъ въ тѣни. Отрадный сонъ
Сомкнулъ глаза невольно мнѣ...
И снова видѣлъ я во снѣ
Грузинки образъ молодой.   395
И странной, сладкою тоской
Опять моя заныла грудь.
Я долго силился вздохнуть—

И пробуди́лся. Ужъ луна́
Вверху́ сія́ла, и одна́   400
Лишь ту́чка кра́лася за ней,
Какъ за добы́чею свое́й,
Объя́тья жа́дныя раскры́въ.
Міръ тёменъ былъ и молчали́въ;
Лишь серебри́стой бахромо́й   405
Верши́ны цѣпи снѣгово́й
Вдали́ сверка́ли пре́до мной,
Да въ берега́ плеска́лъ пото́къ.
Въ знако́мой са́клѣ огонёкъ
То́ трепета́лъ, то́ сно́ва гасъ: 410
На небеса́хъ въ полно́чный часъ
Такъ га́снетъ я́ркая звѣзда́!
Хотѣлось мнѣ... но я туда́
Взойти́ не смѣлъ. Я цѣль одну́,
Пройти́ въ роди́мую страну́,   415
Имѣлъ въ душѣ—и превозмо́гъ
Страда́нье го́лода, какъ могъ.
И вотъ доро́гою прямо́й
Пусти́лся, ро́бкій и нѣмо́й;
Но ско́ро въ глубинѣ лѣсно́й   420
Изъ ви́ду го́ры потеря́лъ
И тутъ съ пути́ сбива́ться сталъ.

XV.

«Напра́сно, въ бѣшенствѣ, порой
Я рвалъ отча́янной руко́й
Терно́вникъ, спу́танный плющёмъ: 425
Всё лѣсъ былъ, вѣчный лѣсъ круго́мъ,
Страшнѣй и гу́ще ка́ждый часъ;

И милліо́номъ чёрныхъ глазъ
Смотрѣ́ла но́чи темнота́
Сквозь вѣ́тви ка́ждаго куста́...　　　430
Моя́ кружи́лась голова́.
Я сталъ влѣза́ть на дерева́;
Но да́же на краю́ небе́съ
Всё тотъ же былъ зубча́тый лѣсъ.
Тогда́ на зе́млю я упа́лъ　　　435
И въ изступле́ніи рыда́лъ
И грызъ сыру́ю грудь земли́,
И слёзы, слёзы потекли́
Въ неё горя́чею росо́й...
Но, вѣрь мнѣ, по́мощи людско́й　　　440
Я не жела́лъ... Я былъ чужо́й
Для нихъ навѣ́къ, какъ звѣрь степно́й;
И е́сли бъ хоть мину́тный крикъ
Мнѣ измѣни́лъ—кляну́сь, стари́къ,
Я бъ вы́рвалъ сла́бый мой язы́къ.　　　445

XVI.

«Ты по́мнишь, въ дѣ́тскіе года́
Слезы́ не зналъ я никогда́;
Но тутъ я пла́калъ безъ стыда́.
Кто ви́дѣть могъ? Лишь тёмный лѣсъ,
Да мѣ́сяцъ, плы́вшій средь небе́съ!　　　450
Озарена́ его́ лучёмъ,
Покры́та мо́хомъ и песко́мъ,
Непроница́емой стѣно́й
Окружена́, передо мной
Была́ поля́на. Вдругъ по ней　　　455
Мелькну́ла тѣнь, и двухъ огне́й

Промчáлись и́скры... и потóмъ
Какóй-то звѣрь одни́мъ прыжкóмъ
Изъ чáщи вы́скочилъ и лёгъ,
Игрáя, нáвзничь на песóкъ.   460
Тó былъ пусты́ни вѣчный гость—
Могýчій барсъ. Сырýю кость
Онъ грызъ и вéсело визжáлъ;
Тó взоръ кровáвый устремля́лъ,
Мотáя лáсково хвостóмъ,   465
На пóлный мѣсяцъ—и на нёмъ
Шерсть отливáлась серебрóмъ.
Я ждалъ, схвати́въ рогáтый сукъ,
Минýту би́твы; сéрдце вдругъ
Зажглóся жáждою борьбы́   470
И крóви; да, рукá судьбы́
Меня́ велá ины́мъ путёмъ...
Но ны́нче я увѣренъ въ томъ,
Что быть бы могъ въ краю́ отцóвъ
Не изъ послѣднихъ удальцóвъ.   475

XVII.

«Я ждалъ. И вотъ въ тѣни́ ночнóй
Врагá почýялъ онъ, и вой
Протя́жный, жáлобный какъ стонъ,
Раздáлся вдругъ... и нáчалъ онъ
Серди́то лáпой рыть песóкъ,   480
Всталъ на дыбы́, потóмъ прилёгъ,
И пéрвый бѣшеный скачóкъ
Мнѣ стрáшной смéртію грози́лъ...
Но я его́ предупреди́лъ.
Удáръ мой вѣренъ былъ и скоръ.   485

Надёжный сукъ мой, какъ топо́ръ,
Широ́кій лобъ его́ разсѣ́къ...
Онъ застона́лъ, какъ человѣ́къ,
И опроки́нулся. Но вновь—
Хотя́ лила́ изъ ра́ны кровь   490
Густо́й, широ́кою волно́й—
Бой закипѣ́лъ, смерте́льный бой!

XVIII.

«Ко мнѣ́ онъ ки́нулся на грудь;
Но въ го́рло я успѣ́лъ воткну́ть
И та́мъ два ра́за поворну́ть   495
Моё ору́жье... Онъ завы́лъ,
Рвану́лся изъ послѣ́днихъ силъ,
И мы, сплетя́сь какъ па́ра змѣ́й,
Обня́вшись крѣ́пче двухъ друзе́й,
Упа́ли ра́зомъ, и во мглѣ́   500
Бой продолжа́лся на землѣ́.
И я былъ стра́шенъ въ э́тотъ мигъ;
Какъ барсъ пусты́нный, золъ и дикъ,
Я пламенѣ́лъ, визжа́лъ, какъ онъ:
Какъ бу́дто самъ я былъ рождёнъ   505
Въ семе́йствѣ ба́рсовъ и волко́въ
Подъ свѣ́жимъ по́логомъ лѣсо́въ.
Каза́лось, что слова́ люде́й
Забы́лъ я—и въ груди́ мое́й
Роди́лся тотъ ужа́сный крикъ,   510
Какъ бу́дто съ дѣ́тства мой язы́къ
Къ ино́му зву́ку не привы́къ.
Но врагъ мой сталъ изнемога́ть,
Мета́ться, ме́дленнѣй дыша́ть,

Сдави́лъ меня́ въ послѣ́дній разъ... 515
Зрачки́ его́ недви́жныхъ глазъ
Блесну́ли гро́зно—и пото́мъ
Закры́лись ти́хо вѣ́чнымъ сномъ;
Но съ торжеству́ющимъ враго́мъ
Онъ встрѣ́тилъ смерть лицо́мъ къ лицу́, 520
Какъ въ би́твѣ слѣ́дуетъ бойцу́!...

XIX.

«Ты ви́дишь на груди́ мое́й
Слѣды́ глубо́кіе когте́й;
Ещё они́ не заросли́
И не закры́лись; но земли́ 525
Сыро́й покро́въ ихъ освѣ́житъ
И смерть навѣ́ки заживи́тъ.
О нихъ тогда́ я позабы́лъ,
И, вновь собра́въ оста́токъ силъ,
Побрёлъ я въ глубинѣ́ лѣсно́й... 530
Но тще́тно спо́рилъ я съ судьбо́й:
Она́ смѣя́лась на́до мной!

XX.

«Я вы́шелъ и́зъ лѣ́су. И вотъ
Просну́лся день, и хорово́дъ
Свѣти́лъ напу́тственныхъ исче́зъ 535
Въ его́ луча́хъ. Тума́нный лѣсъ
Заговори́лъ. Вдали́ ау́лъ
Кури́ться на́чалъ. Сму́тный гулъ
Въ долинѣ́ съ вѣ́тромъ пробѣжа́лъ...
Я сѣлъ и вслу́шиваться сталъ; 540

Но смолкъ онъ вмѣстѣ съ вѣтеркомъ.
И кинулъ взоры я кругомъ:
Тотъ край, казалось, мнѣ знакомъ.
И страшно было мнѣ—понять
Не могъ я долго, что опять   545
Вернулся я къ тюрьмѣ моей;
Что безполезно столько дней
Я тайный замыселъ ласкалъ,
Терпѣлъ, томился и страдалъ,
И всё зачѣмъ?... Чтобъ въ цвѣтѣ лѣтъ, 550
Едва взглянувъ на Божій свѣтъ,
При звучномъ ропотѣ дубравъ
Блаженство вольности познавъ,
Унесть въ могилу за собой
Тоску по родинѣ святой,   555
Надеждъ обманутыхъ укоръ
И вашей жалости позоръ!...
Ещё въ 'сомнѣнье погружёнъ,
Я думалъ—это страшный сонъ...
Вдругъ дальній колокола звонъ   560
Раздался снова въ тишинѣ—
И тутъ всё ясно стало мнѣ...
О, я узналъ его тотчасъ!
Онъ съ дѣтскихъ глазъ ужé не разъ
Сгонялъ видѣнья сновъ живыхъ   565
Про милыхъ ближнихъ и родныхъ,
Про волю дикую степей,
Про лёгкихъ, бѣшеныхъ коней,
Про битвы чудныя межъ скалъ,
Гдѣ всѣхъ одинъ я побѣждалъ!...   570
И слушалъ я безъ слёзъ, безъ силъ.
Казалось, звонъ тотъ выходилъ

Изъ сéрдца—бýдто ктó нибýдь
Желѣзомъ ударя́лъ мнѣ въ грудь.
И смýтно пóнялъ я тогдá,   575
Что мнѣ на рóдину слѣдá
Не проложи́ть ужъ никогдá.

XXI.

«Да, заслужи́лъ я жрéбій мой!
Могýчій конь, въ степи́ чужóй
Плохáго сбрóсивъ сѣдокá,   580
На рóдину издалекá
Найдётъ прямóй и крáткій путь...
Чтó я предъ нимъ?—Напрáсно грудь
Полнá желáньемъ и тоскóй:
Тó жаръ безси́льный и пустóй,   585
Игрá мечты́, болѣзнь умá.
На мнѣ печáть свою́ тюрьмá
Остáвила... Такóвъ цвѣтóкъ
Темни́чный: вы́росъ одинóкъ
И блѣденъ онъ межъ плитъ сыры́хъ;   590
И дóлго ли́стьевъ молоды́хъ
Не распускáлъ, всё ждалъ лучéй
Живи́тельныхъ. И мнóго дней
Прошлó, и дóбрая рукá
Печáлью трóнулась цвѣткá,   595
И былъ онъ въ садъ перенесёнъ,
Въ сосѣдство розъ. Со всѣхъ сторóнъ
Дышáла слáдость бытія́...
Но что жъ? Едвá взошлá заря́,
Паля́щій лучъ ея́ обжóгъ   600
Въ тюрьмѣ воспи́танный цвѣтóкъ.

XXII.

«И, какъ его, палилъ меня
Огонь безжалостнаго дня.
Напрасно пряталъ я въ траву
Мою усталую главу: 605
Изсохшій листъ ея вѣнцомъ
Терновымъ надъ моимъ челомъ
Свивался—и въ лицо огнёмъ
Сама земля дышала мнѣ.
Сверкая быстро въ вышинѣ,   610
Кружились искры; съ бѣлыхъ скалъ
Струился паръ. Міръ Божій спалъ,
Въ оцѣпенѣніи глухомъ,
Отчаянья тяжёлымъ сномъ.
Хотя бы крикнулъ коростель,   615
Иль стрекозы живая трель
Послышалась, или ручья
Ребячій лепетъ... Лишь змѣя,
Сухимъ бурьяномъ шелестя,
Сверкая жёлтою спиной,   620
Какъ будто надписью златой
Покрытый до-низу клинокъ,
Браздя разсыпчатый песокъ,
Скользила бережно; потомъ,
Играя, нѣжася на нёмъ,   625
Тройнымъ свивалася кольцомъ;
То, будто вдругъ обожжена,
Металась, прыгала она
И въ дальнихъ пряталась кустахъ.

XXIII.

«И бы́ло всё на небеса́хъ   630
Свѣтло́ и ти́хо. Сквозь пары́
Вдали́ чернѣли двѣ горы́.
Нашъ монасты́рь изъ-за одно́й
Сверка́лъ зубча́тою стѣно́й.
Внизу́ Ара́гва и Кура́,   635
Обви́въ каймо́й изъ серебра́
Подо́швы свѣжихъ острово́въ,
По ко́рнямъ ше́пчущихъ кусто́въ
Бѣжа́ли дру́жно и легко́...
До нихъ мнѣ бы́ло далеко́!   640
Хотѣлъ я встать—передо мной
Всё закружи́лось съ быстрото́й;
Хотѣлъ крича́ть—язы́къ сухо́й
Беззву́ченъ и недви́жимъ былъ...
Я умира́лъ. Меня́ томи́лъ   645
Предсме́ртный бредъ.
         Каза́лось мнѣ,
Что я лежу́ на вла́жномъ днѣ
Глубо́кой рѣчки—и была́
Круго́мъ таи́нственная мгла.
И, жа́жду вѣчную поя́,   650
Какъ лёдъ холо́дная струя́,
Журча́, вливалася мнѣ въ грудь...
И я боя́лся лишь засну́ть—
Такъ бы́ло сла́дко, лю́бо мнѣ...
А на́до мно́ю въ вышинѣ   655
Волна́ тѣсни́лася къ волнѣ,
И со́лнце сквозь хруста́ль волны́
Сія́ло сладостнѣй луны́...

И рыбокъ пёстрыя стада
Въ лучахъ играли иногда.   660
И помню я одну изъ нихъ:
Она привѣтливѣй другихъ
Ко мнѣ ласкалась. Чешуёй
Была покрыта золотой
Ея спина. Она вилась   665
Надъ головой моей не разъ,
И взоръ ея зелёныхъ глазъ
Былъ грустно-нѣженъ и глубокъ...
И надивиться я не могъ:
Ея сребристый голосокъ   670
Мнѣ рѣчи странныя шепталъ,
И пѣлъ, и снова замолкалъ.
Онъ говорилъ:

        «Дитя моё,
Останься здѣсь со мной:
Въ водѣ привольное житьё—   675
И· холодъ и покой.

            *

    «Я созову моихъ сестёръ:
Мы пляской круговой
Развеселимъ туманный взоръ
И духъ усталый твой.   680

            *

    «Усни! постель твоя мягка,
Прозраченъ твой покровъ.
Пройдутъ года, пройдутъ вѣка
Подъ говоръ чудныхъ сновъ.

            *

«О ми́лый мой! не утаю́, 685
Что я тебя́ люблю́,
Люблю́, какъ во́льную струю́,
Люблю́, какъ жизнь мою́...»

———

«И до́лго, до́лго слу́шалъ я;
И мни́лось, звучная струя́ 690
Сливáла ти́хій ро́потъ свой
Съ словáми ры́бки золото́й.
Ту́тъ я забы́лся. Бо́жій свѣтъ
Въ глазáхъ угáсъ. Безу́мный бредъ
Безси́лью тѣ́ла уступи́лъ... 695

XXIV.

«Такъ я найдёнъ и по́днятъ былъ...
Ты остально́е знáешь самъ.
Я ко́нчилъ. Вѣ́рь мои́мъ словáмъ,
Или не вѣ́рь, мнѣ всё равно́.
Меня́ печáлитъ лишь одно́: 700
Мой трупъ холо́дный и нѣмо́й
Не бу́детъ тлѣ́ть въ землѣ́ родно́й,
И по́вѣсть го́рькихъ му́къ мои́хъ
Не призовётъ межъ стѣ́нъ глухи́хъ
Внимáнье ско́рбное ни чьё 705
На и́мя тёмное моё.

XXV.

«Прощáй, отéцъ... дай ру́ку мнѣ:
Ты чу́вствуешь, моя́ въ огнѣ́...

Знай, э́тотъ пла́мень, съ ю́ныхъ дней
Тая́ся, жилъ въ груди́ мое́й;   710
Но ны́нѣ пи́щи нѣтъ ему́,
И онъ прожёгъ свою́ тюрьму́,
И возврати́тся вновь къ Тому́,
Кто всѣмъ зако́нной чередо́й
Даётъ страда́нье и поко́й...   715
Но что мнѣ въ томъ? Пуска́й въ раю́,
Въ свято́мъ, заобла́чномъ краю́,
Мой духъ найдётъ себѣ прію́тъ—
Увы́! за нѣ́сколько мину́тъ
Между круты́хъ и тёмныхъ скалъ,   720
Гдѣ я въ ребя́чествѣ игра́лъ,
Я бъ рай и вѣ́чность промѣня́лъ!

XXVI.

«Когда́ я ста́ну умира́ть,
И, вѣрь, тебѣ не до́лго ждать—
Ты перене́сть меня́ вели́   725
Въ нашъ садъ, въ то́ мѣсто, гдѣ цвѣли́
Ака́цій бѣ́лыхъ два куста́...
Трава́ межъ ни́ми такъ густа́,
И свѣ́жій во́здухъ такъ души́стъ,
И такъ прозра́чно золоти́стъ   730
Игра́ющій на со́лнцѣ листъ!
Тамъ положи́ть вели́ меня́.
Сія́ньемъ голуба́го дня
Упью́ся я въ послѣ́дній разъ.
Отту́да ви́денъ и Кавка́зъ!   735
Быть мо́жетъ, онъ съ свои́хъ высо́тъ
Привѣ́тъ проща́льный мнѣ пришлётъ,

Пришлётъ съ прохла́днымъ вѣтерко́мъ...
И близъ меня́ передъ концо́мъ
Родно́й опя́ть разда́стся звукъ!   740
И ста́ну ду́мать я, что другъ
Иль братъ, склони́вшись на́до мной,
Отёръ внима́тельной руко́й
Съ лица́ кончи́ны хла́дный потъ,
И что въ-полго́лоса поётъ   745
Онъ мнѣ про ми́лую страну́...
И съ э́той мы́слью я засну́,
И никого́ не прокляну́!»

NOTES

Most of the abbreviations used will be readily understood: *instr.* stands for the instrumental case, and *loc.* for the locative or prepositional. 'Forbes' refers to Mr Nevill Forbes' *Russian Grammar* (Oxford 1914); 'Boyer' to the *Russian Reader* of Messrs Boyer and Speranski.

Verbs are called perfective or imperfective, in the sense that they belong to the perfective or imperfective aspect.

Мцыри, the Russian title of the poem, is not a Russian word; it is the equivalent, in the Georgian language, for our 'novice,' an aspirant who has not yet taken the monastic vows.

The motto which Lérmontov prefixed is taken from the Old Testament—1st Samuel, c. 14, v. 23. The Russian Bible is written in Old Slavonic, which differs in many ways from modern Russian. In our own translation, the words are:—

"I did certainly taste a little honey...and, lo, I must die."

I.

1—26. *Where the rivers Arágva and Kurá meet, there stand the ruins of an ancient monastery. A single old man may still be seen brushing the dust off the memorial stones, one of which records the surrender of Georgia to the Russian power. Protected by the Russian arms, Georgia enjoyed peace and prosperity thereafter.*

1. лѣтъ: gen. pl. after мно́го.

лѣта́, properly 'summers,' serves also as the pl. of годъ, 'year': два го́да, 'two years'; пять лѣтъ, 'five years.'

тому́ наза́дъ = 'ago': lit. 'backward to that': тому́ alone is sometimes used to express the same thing.

мно́го лѣтъ спустя́ = 'many years later.'

2. с-ливáяс-я : pres. gerund, from с-ливáть-ся, where the prefix с- = 'together.'

The ordinary form of the gerund is с-ливá-ясь, but the poets, when they want an extra syllable, often use the older form : cf. l. 25 опасáяс-я for опасáясь.

3. об-нáвши-сь : past gerund, from об-нáть-ся : -ся (or -сь) in reflexive verbs is a contraction of the reflexive pronoun себя́ ; it is pronounced *sa*, not *sya*.

сестры́ : not nom. plur. (which is сёстры) but gen. sing. : a substantive following два (fem. двѣ), три, or четы́ре, must be in the gen. sing. : cf. l. 727 два кустá: for the origin of this singular idiom, see Forbes, p. 91.

4. струи́, 'the waters' : of this noun the gen. sing. and nom. pl. are identical : these cases are often distinguished by the accent, e.g. стрѣлá, 'arrow,' gen. стрѣлы́, nom. pl. стрѣлы.

Tiflís, the chief town of Transcaucasia, stands on the river Kurá; the Arágva runs into the Kurá to the north of Tiflís and south of the Caucasian range.

6. и ны́нче, 'even today' : ны́нче, ны́нѣ, and ны́не are different forms of the same word, meaning (1) 'in our time,' (2) 'today' : однó ны́нче лýчше двухъ зáвтра, 'one today is better than two tomorrow,' i.e. a bird in the hand is worth two in the bush.

пѣше-хóдъ : the road is too steep for other forms of travel.

7. ворóтъ : gen. of ворóта, pl. neut., a front gate or carriage entry ; дверь is 'a door,' and калúтка 'a wicket-gate.'

8. церкóвный свóдъ : the цéрковь, or chapel, is one of the buildings inside the walls. свóдъ, 'vault,' is often used of the sky as well as of a building: so l. 313.

9. курúт-ся : the reflexive verb is used in this sense : so l. 168 ; but онъ курúтъ, 'he is a smoker.'

нимъ: i.e. свóдомъ.

10. кадúльницъ : gen. pl. with what is called the zero ending : i.e. the case represents the stem with no suffix : this is the normal form in fem. nouns ending in -a : во развáлинъ (l. 14), плитъ (l. 16), from развáлина and плитá.

11. не слы́шно пѣнья, 'no singing is heard': cf. Lérmontov's *Phantom Ship*, l. 9 :

> не слы́шно на нёмъ капитáна,
> не ви́дно матрóсовъ на нёмъ

(no captain is heard on board her, no sailors are visible).

слы́шно is a neuter adj.: the constr. is impersonal, and the complement of an impersonal negative verb is always in the gen.: e.g. у меня́ нѣтъ дéнегъ, 'I have no money,' but у меня́ дéньги, 'I have money.' See n. to l. 250.

въ пóздній часъ, 'at a late hour': въ with acc. = 'at' of time, but 'into' of place.

въ, like къ and съ, does not form a syllable, but coalesces entirely with the following word.

12. моля́щихъ: gen. pl., pres. part. of моли́ть: the reflexive моли́ть-ся is used with the same meaning, but the construction differs: 'I pray to God' is either я молю́ Бóга or я молю́-сь Бóгу.

за насъ, i.e. on behalf of sinful mankind in general.

13. оди́нъ, 'a single': sometimes, but not here, used to represent our indefinite article.

14. стрáжъ, 'guardian': the ordinary form is стóрожъ: but the poets often prefer the Old Slavonic equivalents: some of the commonest of these are—власы́ for вóлосы (hair), глáдъ for гóлодъ, глáсъ for гóлосъ; хлáдъ for хóлодъ; see ll. 51, 239, 308, 605.

полу-живóй : we should rather say 'half-dead,' 'with one foot in the grave.'

15. людьми́, 'by men,' лю́ди being used as the plur. of человѣкъ.

The instr. is regularly used to express agency: see l. 54.

за-бы́тъ: past part. passive of за-бы́ть, 'to forget': за-бы́тый would be more correct here: see n. to l. 19.

16. съ, 'from,' takes the gen., as here; but съ, 'with,' takes the instr., e.g. со мной, 'with me.'

17. которыхъ: gen. pl. governed by на́дпись: this relative pronoun, very common in prose, is rare in poetry and does not occur again in this poem.

18. про́шлой, 'past': so въ про́шломъ году́, 'last year.'

19. у-дручёнъ stands for у-дручённый.

Every adj. and past part. passive has two forms, a longer and a shorter: the longer is properly used, when the adj. or part. is an epithet, e.g. хра́брый во́инъ, 'a brave warrior'; the shorter is used, when it forms the predicate, e.g. во́инъ храбръ, 'the warrior is brave'; so пугли́въ, дикъ, слабъ, ги́бокъ (l. 33) for пугли́вый, ди́кій, сла́бый, ги́бкій.

For metrical convenience, the poets sometimes use the short forms, where they are not strictly correct: so here, and забы́тъ in l. 15.

20. тако́й-то царь, 'some king.' When -то is thus tacked on to a pronoun, or pronominal adj. or adv., it makes it indefinite: e.g. кто́-то, 'someone'; что́-то, 'something.'

царь is freely applied to any ruler, not only to the Russian Tsar.

There is a reference here to a historical fact: in 1799 George XIII, King of Georgia, being hard pressed by the Persians, renounced his crown in favour of the Russian Tsar.

21. Россіи: dat.

22. со-шла́, 'came down': perfective: the imperfective с-ходи́ла = 'was coming down' (l. 355): со-йти́ makes, as its past tense, со-шёлъ, со-шла́, со-шли́.

For the distinction between perfective and imperfective aspects, see Appendix.

23. на Гру́зію: acc., because the verb implies motion: if it were said that God's blessing *rested* on the country, на Гру́зіи (loc.) would be needed.

What the Russians call Gruzia, we call Georgia; to the ancients it was known as Iberia.

24. съ тѣхъ поръ: the gen. pl. is used also in the phrase до сихъ поръ, 'hitherto': for the zero ending, see n. to l. 10.

тѣни : locative after въ, to be distinguished from тѣни, gen. and dat. sing., nom. and acc. pl., of the same word. This loc. is found in fem. nouns ending either in -ь, like тѣнь, or in -iя, like Грузiя ; въ Грузiи, 'in Georgia.'

25. опасá-яс-я : for the termination, see n. to l. 2.

враговъ : gen.: опасáть-ся, like боáть-ся, takes the gen.; and, apart from this, the direct object of the verb in a negative sentence is put in the gen.

26: за грáнью, 'behind a barrier': грань is a rare word, but гранúца, a diminutive with no diminutive sense, very common, esp. in such phrases as жить за гранúцей, 'to live abroad'; ѣхать за гранúцу, 'to travel abroad' (lit. 'beyond the frontier').

II.

27—75. *A Russian officer, riding to Tiflis from the Caucasus, once left a boy at this monastery, a Georgian prisoner of six years old, who was unable to bear the long journey. At first homesick and solitary, the boy learnt the Russian language, was baptised, and intended to become a monk. But he disappeared suddenly one night, was found on the steppe three days later in a dying state, and carried back to the monastery. When the priest came to prepare him for death, he made his confession as follows.*

27: однáжды, 'once.' двáжды, 'twice,' is now used only in arithmetic, e.g. двáжды два четúре, 'twice two is four': elsewhere 'twice' is expressed by два рáза.

28. горъ: gen. pl. with zero ending: see n. to l. 10.

про-ѣзжáлъ, 'was travelling past' on horseback or in a carriage : про-ходúлъ would mean that he travelled on foot.

The verb is imperfective, because it describes a prolonged action: the perfective про-ѣхалъ would mean 'had travelled past.'

29. ребёнка : pronounce *reb-yón-ka* : when Russian e has this sound, it always takes the accent.

Therefore the words in which this sound occurs are not marked here with any accent but with a diaeresis over the e (ё).

онъ вёзъ, 'he carried': if the officer had been walking, нёсъ (from нести) must have been used. Pronounce *vyoss*.

30. тотъ, 'that one,' i.e. the child. Where there is a change of subject, as here, this pron. is often used.

за-не-мóгъ, 'fell sick,' perfective : the imperfective, за-не-могáлъ = 'was ill' : see l. 513.

31. трудóвъ : gen., because the verb which governs it is negatived.

пути́: an irregular masc. noun, declined thus—путь, пути́ (gen. and dat.), путёмъ, пути́; pl. пути́, путéй, путя́мъ, etc.

32. лѣтъ шести́, 'of six years,' i.e. six years old.

пять, шесть and higher numerals are followed by a gen. *plur.*; but 'four years' is четы́ре гóда: see n. to l. 3.

33, 34. The four adjectives are all predicates after онъ бы́лъ, and the short predicative forms are therefore used in each case.

35. въ нёмъ (pronounce *vnyom*), 'in him': after a preposition, н is prefixed to the oblique cases of онъ, онá, онó: e.g. у негó, за нимъ, изъ нихъ.

But the loc. is always governed by a preposition: hence no forms of it are used but нёмъ and нéй.

недýгъ is the subject: the sense alone determines this, as the object may just as well come first in Russian, and the acc. of an inanimate noun such as духъ is identical with the nom.

36. раз-ви́лъ, 'had developed,' perfective: aorist, perfect, and pluperfect have only one Russian form.

37. жáлобъ: gen. pl. with zero ending.

38. томи́л-ся and the three following verbs are all imperfectives, because they describe either a continuous state or a repeated action.

39. вы-летáлъ: the perfective is вы́-летѣлъ: for вы, when prefixed to a perfective, is always accented: thus вы-ходи́лъ, вы́-шелъ = 'he walked out,' in both aspects.

40. знако́мъ, 'by a sign,' is written with an accent by Russians themselves, to distinguish it from знако́мъ, the short form of знако́мый, 'familiar': see l. 543.

41. ти́хо, 'silently': the other meaning, 'slowly,' suits the context less well.

у-мира́лъ = 'was on the way to die.'

42. оди́нъ here is simply our indefinite article.

мона́хъ: though we are not expressly told so, it is clear that this monk belonged to the monastery described above.

43. больна́го (pronounce *bal-náw-va*), 'the sufferer,' the adj. being used as a noun: again l. 73.

въ стѣна́хъ, 'within the walls.'

45. иску́сствомъ, i.e. the medical art.

спасёнъ, not being a predicate, should properly be спасён-ный: see n. to l. 19.

46. чу́ждый, 'strange,' here and in l. 262 takes the gen.: the dat. is commoner.

47. снача́ла, adv., = съ нача́ла, 'from the beginning.'

бѣгалъ, 'used to run': бѣгать and бѣжа́ть are both imperfective verbs, meaning 'to run': but the first is indefinite and the second definite : e.g. отъ же́нщинъ бѣгаетъ = 'he avoids women,' but ма́льчикъ бѣжи́тъ, 'the boy is running (now).'

In verse it is easy to distinguish the two verbs, because every part of бѣгать is accented on the first syllable.

In compounds, the verbs in -бѣга́ть are imperfective, the verbs in -бѣжа́ть perfective; hence при-бѣга́ю = 'I run up,' but при-бѣгу́, 'I shall run up.'

48. без-мо́лвенъ, одино́къ: the short forms of без-мо́лвный and одино́кій.

49. вз-дыха́я: pres. gerund, from вз-дыха́ть.

50. томи́мъ: the short form of томи́мый, pres. part. pass. of томи́ть.

The short forms of *present* participles belong chiefly to poetry.

51. по is governed directly by тоскóй: тоскá по рóдинѣ (loc.) = 'home-sickness.'

сторонѣ́: loc.

сторонá and странá are two forms of the same word: see n. to l. 14: but сторонá has assumed the special meaning 'side.' So головá and главá are the same word, but главá in prose = 'heading' or 'chapter.'

52. при-вы́къ, 'became accustomed,' from при-вы́к-нуть: the -ну- suffix disappears in the past tense: see n. to l. 58.

53. сталъ, 'began.'

стать, perfective itself, cannot be followed by a perfective infinitive: hence сталъ понять is impossible.

чужóй, 'foreign,' with the same meaning as чу́ждый (l. 46).

54. окрещёнъ, 'christened': the verb крести́ть (perfective о-крести́ть) is formed from крестъ, -á, 'a cross.'

The participle here forms the predicate and is therefore properly used in its short form.

святы́мъ отцóмъ, 'by the holy father,' presumably the same monk who had taken him into the monastery.

As a matter of fact, the Georgians were Christians, but their method of baptism might not satisfy the Orthodox Church which requires three successive immersions.

55. не-знакóмъ: the short form of не-знакóмый.

56. хотѣлъ, 'was intending': a common meaning of this verb.

во: before certain combinations of consonants, and in certain phrases (e.g. во весь духъ, 'at full speed'), въ, къ, and съ take the forms во, ко, and со.

57. монáшескій: adjectives, where the ending -ескій is preceded by ш, ж, or ч, are accented on the antepenult.: e.g. дру́жескій, грéческій.

58. какъ, 'when,' refers back to ужé, 'by this time.'

исчéзъ, 'disappeared': the past tense of исчéзнуть is исчéзъ, исчéзла, исчéзло, исчéзли: thus the -ну- suffix disappears.

Note that the past tense of the Russian verb indicates

gender and number—онъ былъ, она́ была́, они́ бы́ли. This is due to the fact that it was once a participle; thus it is analogous to the Latin passive—*captus est, capta est, capti sunt.*

59. осе́нней но́чью, 'on an autumn night.' The instr. can express time when, e.g. днёмъ, 'by day'; весно́й, 'in spring'; о́сенью, 'in autumn.'

60. круго́мъ: the instr. of кругъ, -а, 'a circle,' is used, with a change of accent, as an adv., 'around.'

61. три дня: for the gen. sing., see n. to l. 3.

62. напра́сны: short form, for all genders, in predicate. по-то́мъ = по томъ, 'after that'; hence 'later.'

63. его́ на-шли́ = 'he was found.' This pl. with an indefinite subject is often used where we should have a passive verb in the sing.

64. при-несли́ : the verb shows that the bearers were on foot : otherwise при-везли́ would be used. при-несли́ = *adtulerunt*: as a verbal prefix, при- often has the sense of Latin *ad* : so при-шёлъ, l. 77.

65. The long forms of the adjectives are бле́дный and худо́й.

66. бу́дто = какъ бу́дто (see l. 3), 'as if.'

67. ис-пыта́лъ, 'he had experienced': the three nouns are all acc., governed by the verb.

Russian has no pluperfect: the tense is often, as here, expressed by the past perfective; and уже́ is sometimes added.

68. на, 'in answer to': я от-ве́тилъ на ва́ше письмо́, 'I have replied to your letter.'

69. вялъ: imperfective, as describing a state, not an action.

70. бли́зокъ: the short form of бли́зкій: so ги́бокъ for ги́бкій, and по́лонъ for по́лный (l. 366).

сталъ, 'became': the pres. tense, 'becomes,' is станови́т-ся, станови́ться (note the different accent of the inf.) being imperfective of стать.

71. къ нему́: see n. to въ нёмъ (l. 35).

чернéцъ, 'the monk,' who had befriended him before. The word is derived from чёрный, 'black': comp. мертвéцъ, 'a corpse,' from мёртвый, 'dead.'

73, 74. вы́-слушавъ ('having heard him to the end'), and со-брáвъ ('having collected'), are both past gerunds, from perfective verbs.

73. больнóй is here a noun : see l. 43.

74. при-в-стáлъ, 'raised himself a little.'

при- here, as in при-под-нáть-ся, serves to attenuate the meaning of the verb; в-сталъ would mean that he got right out of bed.

The second prefix -в- is not въ, 'in,' 'into,' but a weakened form of вз-, which denotes motion upward: вз-стать has given place to в-стать.

силъ : gen. pl. with zero ending.

75. такъ, 'as follows.'

говори́лъ, 'proceeded to speak': imperfective: the adv. дóлго could hardly be coupled with a perfective.

III.

76—101. "*I am grateful to you for coming to hear my confession, but it is a useless errand. I am conscious of no sins against my fellow-men that need confession ; and my thoughts it is impossible to convey to others. I have always pined for a life of action and excitement, and cherished a secret longing to escape into the free world outside the convent walls. I confess it now, and I refuse to repent.*"

76. ты…при-шёлъ, 'thou *hast* come here.'

Russian has no separate form for the perfect.

слу́шать, 'to listen to': the inf. is regularly used to express purpose after verbs of motion.

и́с-по-вѣдь, 'a confession'; прó-по-вѣдь, 'a sermon'; зá-по-вѣдь, 'a commandment.'

77. сюдá, 'hither.' English now uses 'here' freely in this sense, but Russian never confuses сюдá and здѣсь.

78. всё: adv.; 'in any case.'

лу́чше, 'it is better.'

(1) When a comparative adj. is the predicate, the comp. of the adv. is regularly substituted, e.g. я былъ моло́же, 'I was younger': see n. to l. 183.

(2) The equivalents of *am, art, are* are always omitted in Russian: есть = 'is' is sometimes expressed: see l. 148. The double form of the adjective makes this omission of the verb possible: e.g. in я старъ, the form shows the meaning to be 'I *am* old,' because otherwise ста́рый would be used.

кто́-нибу́дь is still more indefinite than кто́-то (see n. to l. 20): the first has the sénse of *n'importe qui*, the second of *quelqu'un*.

80. зла: gen., because the verb which governs it is negative.

81. мои́, masc. and neut. pl., must not be confused with мой, masc. sing., or sense and metre will suffer.

дѣла́, pl. of дѣло: this shift of accent is common in neuter nouns: e.g. слова́ми (l. 79) is instr. pl. of сло́во.

82. вамъ refers to the monks in general: the monk who is listening is always addressed as ты, not as вы.

83. мо́жно ль, '*is* it possible?' The interrogative enclitic ли (or ль) serves to mark both direct and indirect questions.

84. жилъ, 'have lived,' in our idiom, though жить is imperfective.

въ плѣну́: after въ and на, a number of masculine nouns form a locative in -у or -ю, e.g. въ аду́, 'in hell,' въ раю́, 'in heaven,' въ саду́, 'in the garden.' The last syllable is always accented, and this serves in most cases to distinguish the loc. from the dat. which also ends in -у: so къ плѣ́ну, l. 52.

Nouns which form this ending are masc. and generally monosyllabic in the nom.

85. жи́зни: gen. sing.: see n. to l. 3. The adj. qualifying such a gen. may be either nom. pl. or gen. pl., but not gen. sing.: 'two big volumes' is either два больши́хъ (so here) то́ма, or два больши́е то́ма.

за однý, 'for a single life.'

87. 'I would have given in exchange, if I had been able.'
бы (or бъ) is an enclitic particle, used in the apodosis of a
conditional sentence: e.g. я бы хотѣлъ, 'I should wish.' If
the condition is, as here, unfulfilled, then бы (or бъ) is used
in the protasis also.

éсли is pronounced *yéss-lee*: Russian с is never pronounced
like *z*: hence German *s* is transliterated by з in such names as
Луйза, Зённенбергъ, etc.

90. во мнѣ, 'in me': со ко мнѣ, 'to me,' со мной, 'with
me': in each case the preposition takes the form in -о.

жилá: the fem. of the past tense, if disyllabic, is apt to
accent the last syll.: cf. звалá (l. 92).

91. дýшу, from nom. душá: a number of fem. nouns throw
back the accent in the accusative, e.g. рукá, рýку; водá, вóду;
головá, гóлову.

со-жглá : с-жечь, perfective of с-жигáть, makes, as its past
tense, с-жёгъ, со-жглá, со-жглó.

93. кéлій must be distinguished from кéлии : the first is
gen. pl. and disyllabic ; the second is gen. dat. or loc. sing.
and has three syllables.

94. тотъ, 'that,' is the pronoun of the remote object; hence
тотъ свѣтъ = 'the next world.'

мíръ, 'world,' is thus spelt, to distinguish it from миръ,
'peace': this is the only case in which i is used before a con-
sonant.

95. прáчут-ся : note that if a verb is accented, like прá-
тать, on the 1st syll. in the inf., every form of the verb retains
the accent on that syllable.

скалы́ : nom. plur. : see n. to струй́ (l. 4): the accentuation
скáлы is also found.

96. лю́ди вóльны, 'men *are* free': 'free men' would be
лю́ди вóльные.

99. её, 'it,' i.e. the passion, страсть being fem. её is pronounced *ye-yó*, and ей́ (gen. of онá) has the same sound.

землёй, instr. of земля́, is pronounced землёй.

100. я при-зна́ю, 'I confess': the pres. sense shows that the verb is imperfective : the same form, with a change of accent, is perfective, я при-зна́ю, 'I shall confess' : the respective infinitives are при-знава́ть and при-зна́ть.

101. не молю́, 'I do not pray': 'I shall not pray' would be не по-молю́, the pres. of the perfective.

IV.

102—127. "*Though you saved my life, you did me no kindness. I grew up a solitary child, with no natural relations such as other children have. I vowed that I would at some time, if only for a moment, press a kindred heart to mine. That dream is now over, and I must die, as I have lived, a slave and an orphan.*"

102. я слы́шалъ, 'I have heard.'

слы́шать, 'to hear,' is distinct from слу́шать, 'to listen to' (l. 76): a deaf man is capable of the second, but not of the first, which implies that the sound is caught, not merely listened for: in Russian, глухо́й и слу́шаетъ, да не слы́шитъ. Tolstói, describing his college life, speaks of the lectures, кото́рые я слу́шалъ и изъ кото́рыхъ я не слы́шалъ ни одного́ (at which I was present but to none of which I attended).

мно́го разъ (pronounce *rass*), 'many times': ни ра́зу, 'not even once.'

разъ is an irreg. gen. pl.; the regular form разо́въ is sometimes used.

103. спасъ: the past tense of спасти́ is спасъ, спасла́, спасло́, спасли́.

104. The adjectives, not being predicates, should properly have their long forms, угрю́мый and одино́кій.

105. от-о́-рванный, 'severed' : past part. pass. of от-о-рва́ть, of which the imperfective is от-рыва́ть.

106. вы́-росъ: for the accent, see n. to l. 39.

107. душо́й, 'in heart'; судьбо́й, 'by destiny.'

108. Although нико́му is a negative, the verb is negatived as well; and this is the rule in Russian, e.g. изъ нихъ никто́ не поги́бъ, 'of them not one was lost.'

109. слов: gen., because the verb which governs it is negatived.

сло́во, like most neuter nouns in -о, has the zero ending in the gen. plur.; thus лѣ́то makes лѣ́тъ (l. 1).

оте́цъ and мать are apparently vocatives.

111. чтобъ я = что бы я, 'that I should.'

Note that бы can never be used with the pres. tense, but only with the past or infinitive.

оби́тели: loc. sing. of оби́тель.

113. напра́сно, 'in vain': i.e. the monk's wish was not realised.

звукъ ихъ, 'their sound.' 'Their' can also be expressed by свой, but only where it refers to the subject of the sentence: in such a sentence as они́ по-теря́ли свои́ де́ньги (they lost their money), ихъ де́ньги would be wrong.

рождёнъ: short, predicative, form of рождённый, past part. pass. of роди́ть.

114. ви́дѣлъ, 'used to see.'

One of the commonest uses of the imperfective is to denote repeated action.

у други́хъ, 'belonging to others.' Our 'I have' is generally expressed in Russian by this preposition: у меня́ оте́цъ и мать, 'I have a father and mother.'

115. друзе́й, родны́хъ are not genitives but acc. pl.

In the case of animate nouns, the acc., sing. and pl., has the same form as the gen.: e.g. 'I saw your boys in the street' is я уви́дѣлъ ва́шихъ ма́льчиковъ на у́лицѣ; 'the Sultan loves his wives,' султа́нъ лю́битъ свои́хъ жёнъ.

But a *fem.* animate noun in -а has -у in the acc. sing.: e.g. жена́ makes жену́, and А́нглія makes А́нглію.

But дом, being inanimate, has the same form for nom. and acc. sing., and the same form (дома) for nom. and acc. pl.

116. у себя, 'belonging to myself.'

Note that себя (and свой) are freely used of the 1st and 2nd persons, as well as of the 3rd: e.g. я живу въ своёмъ домѣ, а онъ въ своёмъ, 'I live in my house, and he in his'; не по себѣ дерево не руби, 'don't fell a tree too big for you,' i.e. cut your coat according to your cloth.

117. могилъ: gen. pl., governed by не на-ходилъ. The meaning is—not only did I fail to find dear ones; I could not even find their graves, which most orphans can do.

118. тратя: pres. gerund of тратить.

119. про-из-нёсъ, 'pronounced': чистое про-из-ношеніе, 'a correct pronunciation.'

The following lines explain what this oath was.

120. хотя = 'at least.'

Originally the pres. gerund of хотѣть, 'to wish,' the word is now used with two meanings: (1) although; (2) at least.

когда нибудь, 'at some time or other': see n. to l. 78.

121. пылающую: acc. sing. fem., pres. part. act. of пылать.

122. при-жать, perfective, is used here because the pressure is to be momentary (на мигъ); the imperfective при-жимать would not express this.

съ тоской, lit. 'from misery,' i.e. 'in my misery': so пить съ горя = to drown sorrow in drink.

другой, dat. fem., agreeing with груди.

123. хоть, 'though,' a weakened form of хотя. но, 'yet.'

124. мечтанья тѣ, 'those past dreams.'

мечтанія is an alternative spelling, which contains one more syllable. In this and similar cases (e.g. смертью and смертію), the poets choose whichever form is metrically convenient.

125. по-гибли, 'have been destroyed.'

по-гибнуть, perfective of гибнуть, makes as its past tense, по-гибъ, по-гибла (f.), по-гибло (n.), по-гибли (pl. of all genders). Just so онъ при-вы́къ, 'he was accustomed,' but она́ при-вы́кла, они́ при-вы́кли.

127. у-мру́, 'shall die,' pres. of the perfective у-мере́ть: я у-мира́ю = 'I am dying.'

рабо́мъ, 'as a slave.'

A common and characteristic use of the instrumental: seen in such phrases as я былъ тогда́ ребёнкомъ, 'I was then a child'; слёзы ея́ ли́лись рѣко́й, 'her tears flowed like a river'; служи́лъ онъ въ а́рміи полко́вникомъ, 'he was serving in the army as colonel.'

V.

128—149. "*I have no fear of death, but it gives me pain to part with life so soon. You are old and have forgotten, if you ever had them, the stormy feelings of youth. But at least you have lived, and I might have lived too!*"

129. говоря́тъ, 'men say,' 'it is said.'

спитъ: спать, 'to sleep,' has as its present tense сп-л-ю, спишь, спитъ, спимъ, спите, спятъ.

131. жаль мнѣ, 'I am sorry.'

жаль, originally a fem. noun, has come to be used adverbially. The phrase can govern an acc.: мнѣ жаль бы́ло тебя́, 'I was sorry for you.'

132. я мо́лодъ, 'I *am* young': the adj. is shown by its form to be predicate; the attributive form is молодо́й.

133. раз-гу́льной, 'random,' 'noisy.'

гуля́ть, 'to stroll,' is often used to denote disorderly conduct and especially drunkenness.

134, 135. ты must be supplied as subject of all the four verbs.

135. не-на-ви́дѣлъ и люби́лъ, 'thou wert wont to love and hate.' Both verbs are imperfectives and denote repeated action.

136. би́лося for the usual би́лось: see n. to l. 2.

живѣй, 'quicker': the normal form of the comparative adv. is живѣе, but the poets use the disyllabic form when it suits their metre.

138. съ, 'from,' follows close upon видѣ in l. 137. For the башни of the monastery, see l. 8.

139. свѣжъ: predicative form of свѣжій.

141. The pigeon was not bred there but an immigrant from some far country.

142. при-жа́вшись: past gerund of при-жа́ться. The prefix при- has here the sense explained at l. 64.

144, 145. 'Let the beautiful world be by now distasteful to you': if so, what does it matter?

The 3rd pers., sing. and pl., of the imperative is expressed by пусть or пуска́й (imperatives of пусти́ть and пуска́ть), followed by a 3rd pers. of pres. ind., which may be either imperfective or perfective: e.g. пусть ти́хо спитъ геро́й, 'let the hero sleep in peace'; пуска́й за-бу́детъ свѣтъ его́, 'let the world forget him.'

посты́лъ is the predicative form of the adj. посты́лый, 'distasteful'; the verb (есть, 'is') is omitted.

For the omission of the verb, and for the whole phrase, comp. Púshkin's *Angelo*, III, 2, where Angelo is speaking of Mariana's reputation:

пуска́й себѣ́ молви́ непра́во обвине́нье,
нѣтъ ну́жды. Не должно́ косну́ться подозрѣ́нье
къ супру́гѣ Ке́саря.

'Let the accusation of rumour be unfair—it does not matter. Suspicion must not attach to Caesar's wife.'

сѣдъ: the predicative form of сѣдо́й.

146. жела́ній: gen. pl., of three syllables.

147. что за нужда́, 'what matter is that?'

When что за is used in the sense of како́й, кака́я, the noun which follows за is in the nom.

жилъ, 'hast lived': the past imperfective here corresponds to our perfect.

148. Even if there is nothing in the world which you feel strongly about, at least you have something to forget: you have at least a past, and I have not.

есть does not occur again in the poem: see n. to l. 78.

чтò is often accented thus in Russian texts, to show that it is used as a relative pronoun.

VI.

150—183. "*What did I see, during my days of freedom? I saw fields and tree-crowned hills; I saw dark boulders, divided for ever by streaming mountain torrents; I saw mountain peaks and clouds, like white birds, streaming through the sky; I saw in the distance the snowy Caucasus, and my heart told me that there was my former home. Then the past began to rise clear before me.*"

150. хóчешь: хотѣ́ть, an irregular verb, forms its pres tense thus—хочу́, хóчешь, хóчетъ, хоти́мъ, хоти́те, хотя́тъ.

151. на вóлѣ, 'in freedom,' i.e. when I was free.

153. раз-рóсших-ся, 'spreading': gen. pl. neut., past part. of the reflexive раз-рости́-сь.

As prefix, раз- often implies expansion or separation.

154. шумя́щій is the pres. part. of шумѣ́ть.

толпóй, 'in a crowd.'

155. братъ, 'brother,' makes an irregular pl., бра́тья, бра́тьевъ.

"A brotherhood of lofty elms," says Wordsworth (*Excursion*, I, 29). But dancing seems more appropriate to daffodils.

156. гру́да, 'a heap,' must be distinguished from грудь, 'breast.'

157. ихъ раз-дѣля́лъ, 'was separating them,' i.e. was flowing between them.

ихъ is the acc. pl. (and also gen. pl.) of all three genders.

158. дýмы ихъ, 'their thoughts.' своѝ дýмы would here mean 'my thoughts' : see n. to l. 116.

159. тó, 'that,' i.e. that power. Comp. Púshkin, *Onégin*, п, 31 :

привы́чка свы́ше намъ данá,

замѣ́на счáстію онá—

(habit is given us by heaven, it is a substitute for happiness).

160. про-стёрты, '*are* stretched out.'

With this sense the verb often has an additional suffix : e.g. орёлъ рас-про-стёръ кры́лыл, 'the eagle stretched out his wings.'

162. встрѣ́чи : gen. sing. : most verbs expressing desire take a gen. : e.g. желáю вамъ всегó лýчшаго, 'I send you my best wishes.'

кáждый мигъ : acc. of time, used with or without въ preceding it.

163. бѣгýтъ : бѣжáть, an irregular verb, forms its pres. tense thus—бѣгý, бѣжи́шь, бѣжи́тъ, бѣжи́мъ, бѣжи́те, бѣгýтъ.

164. 'They can never meet.'

имъ : dat. pl.

со-йти́ть-ся is another way of spelling со-йти́-сь. The reflexive is used, as often, to denote the two sides of the action : so стучáть = 'to knock,' but стучáть-ся 'to knock' expecting an answer.

Russian úses the inf. with a dative very freely: comp. ll. 386, 577, 724, and such phrases as не видáть мнѣ тебя́, 'I shall not see you again': nor is the negative indispensable : быть бýрѣ = 'there will be a storm.'

166. причýдливые, 'fantastic' in their outlines.

167. ýтренней, not ýтренной: most adjectives of time and season have 'soft' terminations, e.g. ýтренній, вечéрній, весéнній, лѣ́тній, осéнній, зи́мній, рáнній, пóздній : дáвный, 'of long ago,' used sometimes to be spelt дáвній.

168. кури́ли-ся = кури́ли-сь: see n. to l. 2. Vapour is rising from the summits.

169. голубо́мъ, lit. 'pigeon-coloured,' i.e. light blue : the midnight sky is си́ній, 'dark blue.'

170. за, 'following.' я за нимъ = 'I followed him,' without any verb expressed.

171. по-ки́нувъ : past gerund of по-ки́нуть; like all gerunds, indeclinable : the past part., по-ки́нувшее, would be identical in meaning.

172. на-правля́ло бѣгъ, 'was directing its course': the perfective form, на-пра́вило, has the accent on a different syllable.

173. какъ бу́дто = 'like': comp. l. 3.

карава́нъ, commonly used of a train of camels, may be applied to a line of birds, or carts, or boats.

175. вдали́ : an adv. formed from въ дали́, 'in the distance.'

176. горя́щихъ : loc. pl. masc., pres. part. of горѣ́ть.

178. бы́ло се́рдцу...легко́, 'my heart felt light': this use of the neuter adj. is common, e.g. мнѣ сты́дно, 'I am ashamed'; хорошо́ ли вамъ, 'are you comfortable?'

181. нѣ́-когда, 'at one time,' not to be confused with ни-когда́, 'never,' or иногда́, 'sometimes.'

и я, 'I also.'

жилъ, 'used to live': imperfective.

182. ста́ло, 'became'; стано́вится, 'becomes.'

183. про-ше́дшее: a neut. participle used as a noun: comp. бу́дущее = 'the future.'

яснѣ́й, 'clearer': in the predicate, the comparative adv. is regularly used for the comparative adj.: see n. to l. 78: cf. Púshkin, *Onégin*, viii, 43 :

> Онѣ́гинъ, я тогда́ моло́же,
> я лу́чше, ка́жется, была́

(Onégin, I was younger then; I was fairer, I suppose).

For the ending -ѣ́й instead of -ѣе, see n. to l. 136.

VII.

184—218. "*I recalled an evening scene in my native village —the droves of horses coming home, the dogs barking, the old men sitting near my father's door, and my father himself, the dignified chief in full armour. I remembered my sisters singing over my cradle, a stream that ran through our valley, and tales of the past that were repeated before the evening fire.*"

184. вс-пóмнилъ, perfective, but пóмнилъ, imperfective, in l. 190: 'called to mind' and 'had in mind' may represent the different aspects.

186. раз-сńпанный : the prefix has here the sense of dispersion : see n. to l. 153.

The mountains throw the valley into shade in the afternoon.

187. мнѣ слńшался, 'was audible to me.'

гулъ denotes a distant hollow sound : the Russian for 'sound' is звукъ, but the language is rich in expressions for varieties of sounds : шумъ, for instance, denotes the noise of water or waving trees, while гамъ would describe a hubbub of voices; for звонъ, see n. to l. 201.

188. домóй, 'homewards': but дóма, 'at home.'

бѣгýщихъ : pres. part. of бѣжáть (not of бѣгать, which makes бѣгающій).

189. псовъ : gen. pl. of пёсъ, пса; so ротъ, рта, 'mouth'; лобъ, лба, 'forehead.'

190. старикóвъ : acc. pl.: see n. to l. 115.

192. крыльцá : крыльцó = French *perron*, steps outside a house, which seem an indispensable part of a Russian dwelling and serve as a balcony or veranda.

193. сидѣвшихъ, 'seated': acc. pl., agreeing with старикóвъ.

лицá: gen. sing.: the nom. pl. is лńца: see n. to l. 81.

194. ножёнъ: gen. of ножнъ́, which is used only in the plural: шпа́га доро́же ножёнъ, 'the sword is more precious than the scabbard.'

196. сму́тной чередо́й, 'in a dim procession': for this use of the instr., cf. толпо́й (l. 154).

199. въ='wearing'—a common use: so съ with instr. often = 'carrying.'

200. явля́лся: why not the perfective яви́лся? Probably, because the imperfective, like the imperfect tense in Greek and Latin, has a descriptive and dramatic force which the perfective has not: the mind, so to speak, dwells upon the picture.

201. звонъ denotes a metallic sound and especially the sound of church-bells; звона́рь = 'a bell-ringer.'

203. сестёръ: acc. pl., governed by по́мнилъ: both лучи́ and звукъ below are governed by по́мнилъ.

205. рѣче́й: gen. pl. of рѣчь, рѣчи.

Note that the gen. pl. of hard masc. nouns in -чъ also ends in -ей, e.g. мечъ, 'a sword,' makes мече́й, and лучъ makes луче́й.

207. бѣжа́лъ, 'used to run'; imperfective.

208. шу́менъ and не-глубо́къ are the predicative forms of шу́мный and не-глубо́кій.

209. къ нему́, 'to it,' the stream: for the н prefixed to ему́, see n. to l. 35.

на = 'to get to': if на here meant 'on,' the loc. пескѣ́ would be needed.

210. игра́ть: for the inf. of purpose, comp. слу́шать (l. 76).

въ по́лдень, 'at midday.' In composition, пол- = 'half': cf. въ-полго́лоса (l. 745).

у-ходи́лъ, 'used to go away': the perfective у-шёлъ would mean 'went away' on one particular occasion.

211. ла́сточка, 'a swallow,' being animate, the acc. plur. has the same form as the gen. pl.: hence ла́сточекъ (not ла́сточки) must be used here.

213. волны́: gen. sing.: for каса́ться governs that case.

Note the difference between во́лны (waves) and во́льны (free), l. 96; also the difference between каса́ться (to touch) and каза́ться (to seem).

215. вече́рній and пре́жній below have 'soft' terminations: see n. to l. 167.

216. о томъ, какъ, lit. 'about that, how': the first two words are superfluous in English: cf. l. 18.

VIII.

219—240. "*My escape gave me one taste of life as it goes on outside the convent walls, and the three days were days of bliss to me. I had long wished to look at the free world outside, and I found my chance one stormy night when all you monks were crouching in prayer before the altar. I went out into the night and felt that there was sympathy between my stormy heart and the rage of the elements.*"

220. жилъ, 'I lived,' his life in the convent not being reckoned as life at all but a living death.

221. трёхъ: gen. of три.

три дня is Russian for 'three days': but when a preposition, like безъ here, is followed by the numeral in an oblique case, the noun agrees with the numeral, whatever its case may be. So 'two sisters' is двѣ сестры́, but 'with two sisters' is съ двума́ сестра́ми.

222. была́ бъ, 'would have been': in Russian this is not distinguished from 'would be.'

If an adj. has two syllables, like мра́чный, the adv. shifts its accent in the comparative: thus мра́чно makes мрачнѣ́е; but an adj. of more than two syllables, like печа́льный, has a fixed accent, and makes печа́льно, печа́льнѣе (often, in verse, печа́льнѣй).

223. ста́рости: the gen. is regularly used after the comparative, to express 'than': cf. l. 662.

224. давны́мъ-давно́ : a stronger form of давно́ : in не-
да́вно, 'not long ago,' there is a shift of accent.

225. вз-гляну́ть, 'to take one glance': the suffix -ну-
often denotes unity of action.

226. ли, the interrogative particle, is an enclitic and
therefore cannot stand first in a question, whether direct or
indirect; its usual place is second.

227. тюрьмы́ = imprisonment.

228. на э́тотъ свѣтъ, 'into this world': the next world is
тотъ свѣтъ.

родим-ся, 'we are born': imperfective.   This is one of a few
verbs, in which the perfective and imperfective forms are the
same : in such a sentence as онъ роди́л-ся въ А́нглiи (he was
born in England) the sense is perfective.

229. ужа́сный, formed from у́жасъ (horror), with a shift of
accent.

230. пуга́ла, 'was frightening': imperfective.

васъ refers to all the monks, not only to the monk addressed;
or тебя́ would be used.

231. с-толпи́-сь: pres. gerund, from с-толпи́ть-ся, derived
from толпа́, 'a crowd.'

The prefix с- here = 'together': for another meaning, see n.
to l. 16.

234. об-ня́ть-ся = 'to exchange embraces.'   For this re-
ciprocal meaning of the reflexive, see n. to со-йти́ть-ся (l. 164).

радъ is used only in the predicative form.

236. лови́лъ, 'tried to catch': the imperfective is quite in
place here, as success would have been impossible.

237. скажи́: imperative of сказа́ть.

238. могли́ бы дать вы мнѣ, 'could you have given me,'
'you' being the monks : the order of words is unlike our own
but very like the order in Latin; and this is true of Russian
order in general.

239. кра́ткой : an older form of коро́ткой : see n. to l. 14.

240. се́рдцемъ: мои́мъ is to be supplied.

IX.

241—263. *"There was no starlight to guide me. The fresh
air of the forest was a refreshment to my lungs. When
weary with running, I lay down in the grass and listened
for the sound of pursuers. The storm passed, and a faint
strip of light grew between the earth and sky; I could see
the pattern traced by the distant peaks against the sky.
As I lay, I heard a jackal cry or saw a snake slip past;
but I had no fear of them: I felt like a wild creature
myself."*

241. бѣжа́лъ, 'I kept on running': imperfective.

гдѣ and куда́ are not confused in Russian, as 'where' and
'whither' are in modern English.

243. For the repeated negative (ни...не), see n. to l. 108.

путь: the gen. пути́ would be more usual after the negatived
verb; but the acc. is found, though far less often, in this
position. For another instance, see l. 705.

247. и то́лько, lit. 'and only,' is an idiom, meaning 'that
was enough (for me)': да и то́лько is often used colloquially
with the meaning, 'there's an end of it,' or 'that's flat.'

часо́въ: gen. governed by мно́го: cf. l. 1.

248. у-ста́въ: past gerund, from у-ста́ть.

я у-ста́ну = 'I shall be weary'; я у-ста́лъ = 'I grew weary.'
The imperfective у-става́ть makes у-стаю́, 'I grow weary.'
There is also an adj. у-ста́лый, 'weary': see l. 680.

250. при-слу́шал-ся, 'I listened': the compound reflexive
verb implies deliberate purpose, which слу́шать itself does not:
comp. смотрѣ́ть and при-сма́тривать-ся.

пого́ни нѣ́тъ, 'there is no pursuit,' the negative of есть
пого́ня.

When the substantive verb 'to be' is negatived, the subject
is always in the genitive: e.g. у меня́ нѣ́тъ де́негъ, 'I have no
money'; but 'I have money' is у меня́ де́ньги, or есть у меня́

де́ньги. So его́ тамъ не́ бы́ло, 'he was not there.' Comp. l. 310.

251. у-ти́хла, 'had died away': the perfective here corresponds to our pluperfect: у-тиха́ла (imperfective) would mean 'was dying away.'

252. дли́нной полосо́й, 'in a long strip': for this use of the instr., cf. толпо́й (l. 154).

254. раз-лича́лъ, 'distinguished': раз-, like our 'dis-,' implies separation: see n. to l. 153.

255. на ней, 'on it,' i.e. the strip of light.

зубцы́: pl. of зубе́цъ.

зу́бы, 'teeth,' are the teeth of any animal; зубцы́ is used of inanimate objects, arranged in a row, which resemble an animal's teeth, e.g. the teeth of a wheel or a comb, battlements, pinnacles of mountains.

In the same way спина́ is the back of a living thing; but the back of a chair or a coat is спи́нка.

256. мо́лча, 'in silence,' is thus accented, when it is merely an adverb: originally it was молча́, being a pres. gerund, from молча́ть.

257. уще́лии: the alternative spelling, уще́льи, was used in l. 207.

259. блестя́: pres. gerund, from блесте́ть.

260. камне́й: gen. pl.: межъ (or ме́жду) can govern either gen. as here, or instr. as in l. 240.

ка́мень has two plurals: (1) ка́мни, камне́й; (2) каме́нья, каме́ньевъ.

261. с-жалъ, lit. 'pressed together': comp. с-толпя́сь in l. 231.

262. чуждъ: the predicative form of чу́ждый. This adj. generally takes the dat., so that лю́дямъ would be more normal than the gen. люде́й: but see l. 46.

263. ползъ: ползти́, 'to creep,' has as its past tense ползъ, ползла́, ползло́, pl. ползли́.

X.

264—288. "*Far below me I heard the roar of a mountain torrent, chafing against the rocks that formed its bed; I could understand their angry voices. Then the east began to lighten: a breeze blew, birds began to twitter, and flowers to awake. I looked up, to find that I was lying on the edge of a precipice; the steps that led down to the river below were such as no human foot had ever trod.*"

264. в-низ́, lit. 'in the depth': низ́ is the loc., governed by въ; hence the accent is on the last syllable: see n. to l. 84: с-ни́зу, 'from below,' shows the gen. accent.

266. шумъ: for Russian names of sounds, see n. to l. 187.

267. со́тнѣ. dat. governed by подо́бился.

со́тня is formed from сто (a hundred) like French *centaine* from *cent*.

268. подо́бил-ся = подо́бенъ былъ, 'was like': the adj., подо́бный in its long form, is much commoner than the verb.

269. вня́тенъ: the predicative form of вня́тный.

272. то́...то́ are adverbs: 'at one time,...at another.' с-тиха́лъ and раз-дава́л-ся are imperfectives, as denoting repeated action.

онъ, 'it,' i.e. раз-гово́ръ.

сильнѣ́й: for the accent, see n. to l. 222.

275. за-пѣ́ли, 'began to sing.' Most imperfective verbs that denote sound, form their perfectives by addition of the prefix за-.

The three following verbs are also perfectives, and thus serve to indicate the *sudden* coming of dawn.

277. листъ has two plurals: (1) ли́стья, -тьевъ; (2) листы́, -о́въ: both are used for 'foliage,' but the second is used also for 'leaves' of books, etc.

278. со́нные, 'sleeping.'

цвѣты́, 'flowers': for the sing. 'flower,' the dim. цвѣто́къ is used: see l. 588.

280. го́лову: but nom. голова́: see n. to l. 91.

281. о-смотре́л-ся, 'looked round about': this is the usual sense of о- in composition.

282. мне́ ста́ло стра́шно, 'I felt frightened': for the impersonal construction, see n. to l. 178.

кра́ю: loc. and therefore accented on the last syllable; the dat. of край is кра́ю.

For the loc. in -у́ or -ю́, see n. to l. 84.

283. грозя́щей: gen. sing. fem., pres. part. of грози́ть.

бе́здны: the nom. бе́здна is a formation from безъ дна, 'without bottom,' which has become a fem. noun.

284. вылъ must not be confused with былъ.

крутя́-сь: pres. gerund, from крути́ть-ся.

285. туда́, 'thither'; but от-ту́да, 'thence' (l. 735).

скалъ: gen. pl.

286. злой духъ, 'the Evil Spirit': one of the Russian names for Satan: Dal's Dictionary records thirty-five other titles by which he is called.

по нимъ, 'along them.'

287. съ, 'from,' as the following gen. shows.

XI.

289—321. "*Flowers, wet with rain, grew round me; and vines, laden with clusters of grapes, twined about the trees. Every voice of Nature was raised in praise of the Creator; the voice of man alone was absent. What I thought then I would fain repeat now, but I cannot. I feasted on the stainless purity of the sky till the increasing heat of the day made me thirsty.*"

289. круго́мъ: not *all* round, as he lay on the verge of a precipice.

цвѣлъ is pronounced цвёлъ (*tsvyol*): ѣ seldom has this sound which е generally takes when accented.

290. расте́ній: gen. pl.

ра́дужный, 'rainbow-coloured,' must be distinguished from
раду́шный, 'cordial.'

293. вили́-сь : ви́ть-ся, 'to twine,' has, as its present tense,
вью́-сь, вьёшь-ся, вьёт-ся; the past tense is ви́л-ся, вила́-сь,
вило́-сь, ви́ли-сь : the accent вили́-сь, used here, is not
ordinarily used.

This verb is used to express the spiral flight of birds, the
swimming of a fish (l. 665), the curling of wreaths of dust
(l. 328) or smoke.

краcу́я-сь : pres. gerund, from красова́ть-ся.

Note that verbs in -ова́ть make a present in -у́ю, -у́ешь,
but their past tense ends in -ова́лъ.

294. зе́ленью, instr. after краcу́я-сь.

295. по́лные refers both to size and shape of the clusters.

нихъ, i.e. кудря́ми.

296. серёгъ : серьга́ (ear-ring) makes in the pl. се́рьги,
серёгъ; so деньга́ (coin) makes де́ньги, де́негъ (money).

подо́бье, 'a likeness,' i.e. like : comp. Latin *instar*.

дороги́хъ : дорого́й, 'precious,' must be distinguished from
доро́гой, 'on the way,' instr. of доро́га (l. 418).

297. поро́й, 'at times' : see l. 139.

298. къ нимъ, i.e. to the clusters.

рой is properly a 'swarm' of bees.

300. в-слу́шивать-ся : the simple verb слу́шать takes an
accusative, but the compound reflexive verb requires a different
construction.

Note that стать, itself perfective, is never followed by a
perfective infinitive, such as в-слу́шать-ся : this is true also of
пере-ста́ть, 'to cease.'

302. по куста́мъ, 'through the bushes.'

The rustling of leaves is meant, and the indications of
animal life.

303. какъ бу́дто...вели́, 'as if they were carrying on.'

вели́ : 3rd pers. pl., past tense of вести́.

вести́ and води́ть both mean 'to lead,' and both are imperfectives; the difference in their use is the same as that between бѣжа́ть and бѣ́гать (see n. to l. 47), or between идти́ and ходи́ть.

305. голоса́: irregular pl. of го́лосъ: the gen. sing. is го́лоса.

When masculine nouns form their plural in -a, the -a is always accented. Such instances as глаза́ (eyes) and берега́ (banks) seem to show that this form was once a dual number; but it is now a true plural in the case of го́лосъ and many other nouns.

306. с-лива́ли-сь, 'were mingling': the perfective, с-ли́ли-сь, would mean 'were mingled.'

раз-дал-ся́: the accentuation раз-да́л-ся is also used: see l. 561.

308. гласъ is an older form of го́лосъ: see n. to l. 14.

310. имъ нѣтъ слѣда́, 'there is not a trace of them,' the opposite of есть слѣдъ, 'there is a trace': see n. to l. 250.

имъ: dat. pl.: ихъ, the gen., would be more usual.

311. ихъ: acc. pl.

312. хоть мы́сленно, 'in thought, at least.'

313. въ то у́тро, 'on that morning,' то referring to the past; тотъ can also refer to the future but not to the present, of which э́тотъ is used.

314. такъ чистъ, 'so pure.'

Note that такъ is used only with the predicative form of the adj.: so такъ густа́ (l. 728). 'So pure a vault' is тако́й чи́стый сводъ, both adjectives having the longer form.

по-лётъ (pronounce *pa-lyót*) is acc.

316. онъ, i.e. сводъ.

317. по́лонъ, полна́, полно́ is the predicative form of по́лный, по́лная, по́лное: the shift of accent should be noted.

синево́й: instr.: the gen. would be equally possible.

319. тону́лъ: тону́ть is properly 'to sink'; e.g. ло́дка у-то́нетъ, 'the boat will go down.' But the word is also used metaphorically of vast happiness or good fortune; and a man is said тонуть въ блаженствѣ (to swim in bliss) or въ роскоши (in luxury). This is the sense here.

пока…не, 'until.'

полдневный: an adj. of time with hard terminations, like дневный from which it is formed: see n. to l. 167.

320. мечты: not gen., because пока не is not considered as making the sentence negative.

раз-о-гналъ: perfective, of the completed action: the imperfective is раз-гонялъ.

321. томить-ся: imperfective, as is necessary after сталъ.

XII.

322—352. "*In my thirst I scrambled down the side of the precipice, clinging to bushes and dislodging boulders. I reached the bottom of the terrible descent and hastened to slake my thirst in the stream. A sudden sound made me hide in the bushes; I listened and heard the voice of a Georgian girl coming nearer; the song she was singing still rings in my ears at night.*"

323. держа-сь, 'holding on,' but держа, 'holding' (l. 353): the pres. gerunds of держать-ся and держать.

за, 'by.'

324. съ плиты на плиту, 'from flat stone to flat stone': for the shift of accent in the accusative, see n. to l. 91.

325. спускать-ся началъ: начать is perfective, with imperfective начинать; but, like стать, it takes an imperfective infinitive after it.

The pres. tense of начать is начну, начнёшь (with fut. sense); the past tense is началъ, начала, начало.

изъ-подъ: comp. изъ-за (l. 5).

ногъ: gen. pl.

326. со-рвавши-сь: past gerund, from со-рвать-ся.

327. за нимъ, 'behind it,' 'in its wake.'

бразда: the older spelling of борозда, 'a furrow': see n. to стражъ (l. 14).

328. вил-ся́: ви́л-ся is the usual accent: see n. to l. 293.

столбо́мъ, 'in the form of a pillar.' For this characteristic use of the instr., see n. to l. 127.

329. гудя́, pres. gerund, from гудѣ́ть: пры́гая, pres. gerund, from пры́гать.

Both verbs are imperfective: it should be noted that most perfective verbs (such as за-гудѣ́ть and пры́гнуть) have no present gerund.

330. онъ, i.e. ка́мень.

по-глоща́емъ: nom. sing. masc., pres. part. pass. of по-глоща́ть, in its predicative form.

332. The verse shows clearly the necessity of the double form of Russian adjectives: otherwise it would be impossible to distinguish the subject from the predicate: cf. l. 729.

сильна́, '*is* strong.' Many fem. adjectives, in their predicative form, are accented on the last syllable: e.g. во́льная becomes вольна́, and стра́шная becomes страшна́.

334. лишь то́лько, 'as soon as,' like какъ то́лько: лишь alone is used in this sense in l. 351.

335. с-пусти́л-ся: perfective, of the completed action; but с-пуска́л-ся, imperfective, = 'I was descending.'

336. навстрѣ́чу, i.e. на встрѣ́чу, 'in order to meet': the Latin *obuiam* is formed in the same way, and also takes the dat. after it.

339. с-кры́вши-сь: past gerund, from с-кры́ть-ся.

340. объя́тъ: the predicative form of the participle is not needed here: объя́тый would be normal.

342. в-слу́шивать-ся сталъ: cf. ll. 300, 540.

343. бли́же всё, 'ever nearer.'

бли́же is the comparative of бли́зко: всё is an adv., meaning 'all the time.'

344. Грузи́нка is the fem. of Грузи́нецъ.

молодо́й might be either nom. masc. or gen. fem., the forms being identical; the sense shows it to be the latter.

346. бу́дто онъ, 'as if it...,' i.e. the voice.

348. прі-учёнъ, 'accustomed': стáраго пса къ цѣпи не пріу́чишь, 'you can't accustom an old dog to the chain.'

The predicative form of the participle is in place here.

349. 'That was a simple song.'

Though тó is the subject, yet the verb is fem., agreeing with the predicate: for the same construction, see l. 461. Comp. Púshkin, *Ruslán*, I, тó три сопéрника Руслáна (these were the three rivals of Ruslán).

350. въ мысль…мнѣ, 'into my mind.' онá, 'it.'

351. на-стаётъ, 'begins.'

на-ставáть, imperfective, makes на-стаю́, на-стаёшь, in the present ind.: so давáть (to give) makes даю́, даёшь. The present of the perfective на-стáть is на-стáну, на-стáнешь; and this, like all perfective presents, has a future sense; на-стáнетъ порá, 'the time will come.'

352. её (pronounce *ye-yó*), 'it,' the song.

XIII.

353—390. "*Bearing a pitcher on her head, she came down a narrow slippery path to the stream. She was poorly dressed and sunburnt; but the depth of her dark eyes troubled my heart. She filled her pitcher and went back, stately as a poplar, to her home perched on the hillside. I can still see that door open and shut again. But you cannot understand what I felt: let my secret die with me!*"

354. у́зкою тропóй, 'by a narrow path.'

тропи́нка is the form preferred in prose.

355. с-ходи́ла, 'was coming down': the perfective со-шлá (see l. 22) would mean 'came down' or 'had come down.'

Note that all compounds of ходи́ть are imperfective, and all compounds of идти́ perfective.

357. смѣя́-сь, 'laughing': pres. gerund.

смѣя́ть-ся, 'to laugh at,' may be followed by the dat., as here, or by надъ and the instr. as in l. 532.

358. бѣденъ, бѣдна́, is the predicative form of бѣдный, бѣдная.

ея́ : pronounce *ye-yó*.

359. шла, 'she walked': the simple verb is imperfective.

наза́дъ…отъ-ки́нувъ, 'having thrown back': we say 'with the folds thrown back.'

ки́нуть, 'to throw,' and all its compounds are perfective, while кида́ть and its compounds are imperfective.

360. чадра́ (or ча́дра) is a long white garment worn by women and covering the whole figure.

362. по-кры́ли, 'had covered': по-крыва́ли, imperfective, would mean 'were covering.'

тѣнью, 'with a tinge.'

364, 5. устъ…щёкъ…оче́й are all gen. plur. Prose uses гу́бы for 'lips' and глаза́ for 'eyes.' In Púshkin's verse, the 'cheeks' are generally called лани́ты, not щёки.

365. такъ глубо́къ, 'so deep': but 'such deep darkness' is тако́й глубо́кій мракъ : see n. to l. 314.

366. по́лонъ: see n. to l. 317.

367. мой, pl., has two syllables; мой has one.

369. звонъ shows that the pitcher was made of metal: see n. to l. 187.

370. в-лива́ла-сь, 'was pouring in': the continuous action is described by the imperfective.

въ него́, 'into it.'

371. шо́рохъ, 'a rustling sound,' presumably caused by her dress and movements.

бо́льше ничего́, 'nothing more'; i.e. that is all I remember.

372. же here is something like our 'but.'

373. от-лил-а́, perfective, describes a completed action. We might use the pluperfect.

375. хоть ти́ше, 'although more slowly': she was now going up-hill, and carrying a heavier burden.

ти́ше is the comparative of ти́хо.

но, 'yet.'

376. стройна́, 'stately': predicative form of стро́йная.

379. каза́лось refers to the words that follow: the huts looked as if they had grown on (при-) to the rock. For this sense of при-, see n. to l. 64.

380. са́кли, gen. sing. of са́кля: see n. to дв ѣ сестры́ (l. 3).

дру́жною четой, 'in a friendly pair.'

381. одно́й, gen. sing. agreeing with са́кли understood.

383. бу́дто бы = какъ бу́дто.

384. от-перла́-сь: от-пере́ть (with imperfective от-пира́ть) makes, in the present, от-о-пру́ (I shall open), от-о-прёшь; the past tense is о́т-перъ, от-перла́, о́т-перло.

за-пере́ть (за-пира́ть) is 'to shut.'

385. за-твори́ла-ся: perfective: the imperfective is за-твори́ла сь.

386. теб ѣ́...не поня́ть, 'you cannot understand': see n. to l. 164.

388. могъ: the subject to be supplied is ты.

мн ѣ́ бы́ло бъ жаль, 'I should be sorry' to describe my feelings.

390. во мн ѣ́, 'in me,' i.e. hidden in my breast.

пуска́й у-мру́тъ, 'let...die.' For this construction, see n. to l. 144.

XIV.

391—422. "*I was weary, and sleep overcame me; the image of the Georgian maiden haunted my dreams. When I woke, the moon was shining; I could see the silver fringe of the snow-clad hills, and hear the sound of the torrent; from time to time a light was visible in the maiden's cottage, and tempted me. But my one aim was to find my way to my birthplace. Crushing down the pangs of hunger, I started; but soon I lost my way in the forest.*"

392. я лёгъ, 'I lay down.'

лечь, 'to lie down' (imperfective ложи́ть-ся), makes, in its past tense, лёгъ, легла́, легло́.

393. глаза́ мнѣ́ : we say 'my eyes'; but French would have *me ferma les yeux.*

395. молодо́й : gen. fem.

397. за-ны́ла, 'began to ache': a very common meaning of за- when prefixed to a verb.

398. вз-дохну́ть, 'to fetch a breath.' He seemed to be choking in his dream.

400. вверху́ = въ верху́. The case being locative, the last syllable is accented. Comp. внизу́, l. 264.

401. кра́ла-ся : the past tense of кра́сть-ся is usually accented кра́л-ся, крала́-сь, кра́ло-сь.

за ней, 'behind her.'

403. рас-кры́въ : past gerund, from рас-кры́ть.

404. тёменъ, темна́, темно́ is the predicative form of тёмный, тёмная, тёмное.

405. бахромо́й, 'like a fringe': for this use of the instr., see n. to l. 127.

406. верши́ны is nom. plur., цѣ́пи gen. sing.

408. въ берега́, 'against its banks.'

For this plural of бе́регъ, see n. to l. 305.

409. знако́мой : it was familiar, in the sense that it was inhabited by someone whom he had seen, but not otherwise.

огонёкъ : diminutive of ого́нь, which means either 'a light' or 'a fire': the first is the meaning here.

410. гасъ, га́сла, га́сло is the past tense of га́снуть, 'to go out' (of a light); the pres. tense is га́сну, га́снешь, etc.

411. на небеса́хъ, 'in the heavens.'

не́бо has in the plural небеса́, небе́съ, etc.

413. хотѣ́лось мнѣ́ : an impersonal reflexive construction of a common type: this differs from я хотѣ́лъ, in so far as "it lays less stress on the influence of the person in question on the act itself" (Boyer, p. 248).

Similar phrases are—мнѣ́ ду́мает-ся, 'I am inclined to think'; мнѣ́ не спи́т-ся, 'I am not inclined to sleep.'

414. вз-о-йти́, 'to climb up': the imperfective is вс-ходи́ть.

взо- is another form of вз- or воз-: all signify upward motion.

415. про-йти́, 'to travel along': про- before a verb regularly has the sense of 'along' or 'past,' e.g. боле́знь ско́ро пройдётъ, 'the illness will soon pass': cf. l. 28.

416. пре-воз-мо́гъ, 'overcame': past tense of пре-воз-мо́чь.

417. какъ могъ, 'as best I could.'

418. доро́гою: see n. to l. 296.

421. изъ ви́ду...по-теря́лъ, 'I lost from sight,' i.e. I lost sight of.

Many masculine nouns have an alternative genitive in -y (or -ю): видъ makes ви́ду as well as ви́да; чай (tea) makes ча́ю as well as ча́я.

This gen. can generally be distinguished from the loc. in -y, by means of the accent: thus съ ви́ду = 'in appearance,' but на виду́ = 'in view.'

го́ры: acc. pl.: gen. sing. is горы́.

по-теря́ть is the perfective of теря́ть: 'loss' is по-те́ря, and 'Paradise Lost' is По-те́рянный Рай.

422. съ пути́, 'from the way': 'from' is repeated in the prefix of the verb following.

с-бива́ть-ся: imperfective after сталъ.

XV

423—445. "*Lost in an endless wood, I tried to tear a way through the bushes. I climbed trees to get a view, but in vain. Then I fell on the ground, gnawed the earth, and wept. But even in that dire extremity, I neither desired nor sought human aid; I despised such weakness.*"

424. рвалъ: imperfective of repeated action.

425. терно́вникъ, 'thorn-bushes': the noun has a collective sense: comp. оре́шникъ, 'a hazel copse.'

с-пу́танный: the prefix с- here means 'with' 'together.'

426. всё лѣсъ былъ, 'everywhere there were trees.'

427. The two comparative adverbs are used for adjectives in the predicate: see n. to l. 183.

432. в-лѣзáть, 'to climb up': imperfective after сталъ. In this verb, and in the perfective в-лѣзть, the prefix is not въ (in, into) but a weakened form of вз- (or воз-) which denotes upward motion. The same prefix is similarly disguised in в-стать, 'to stand up,' and many other verbs: see n. to l. 74.

деревá: pl. of дéрево, with the shift of accent usual in these neuter nouns.

433. на краю́, 'on the edge': the horizon is meant.

Note that the loc. in -ю has the accent on the final syllable: the dat. of край is крáю.

434. тотъ же, 'the same.'

зубчáтый: the tops of the trees stick up like rows of teeth. The epithet is more often applied to a wall with battlements: see l. 634.

435. зéмлю: acc. of земля́: see n. to l. 91.

437. грызъ: грызть (to gnaw) has, as pres. tense, грызý, грызёшь, etc., and, as past tense, грызъ, грызла, грызло.

сырýю: it is not meant that the soil was damp: сырáя is a standing epithet of земля́, especially when Earth is personified: comp. l. 526. So какъ егó, грѣшника, мать сырá земля́ нóситъ? (why does good old Mother Earth support such a sinner?).

439. въ неё, 'into it.'

росóй, 'like dew': for this use of the instr., see n. to l. 127.

росá, 'dew,' must be distinguished from рóза, 'a rose.'

440. вѣрь: imperative of вѣрить; pl. вѣрьте.

пóмощи: gen., as object of a negatived verb.

людскóй, 'from men.'

441. чужóй has no predicative form, or it would be used here; but чуждъ is used as well as чýждый: see l. 46.

442. для нихъ, 'as far as they were concerned.'

443. крикъ is a cry for help, not a mere expression of grief; he has confessed that degree of weakness.

444. мнѣ : из-мѣни́ть, 'to betray,' is followed by the dative : жени́къ из-мѣни́лъ ей, 'her lover has been unfaithful to her'; си́лы из-мѣня́ютъ старику́, 'his powers are failing the old man.'

из-мѣни́ть, when it means 'to change,' takes the acc. : из-мѣ́на = 'treason,' while пере-мѣна or из-мѣне́ніе = 'change.'

кляну́-сь : кля́сть-ся (to swear) makes кляну́-сь, клянёшь-ся in the present, and кля́л-ся, клял-а́сь in the past tense.

445. я бъ вы́-рвалъ, 'I would have torn out.'

вы- is always accented, when prefixed to a perfective verb; but the imperfective is вы-рыва́лъ.

сла́бый, 'cowardly.'

The line is too much in the manner of Victor Hugo : the best Russian literature is remarkably free from rhetorical exaggeration.

XVI.

446—475. *"Though I never shed a tear in childhood, I wept now without restraint in my solitude. In front of me there was a clearing in the wood, and suddenly I saw the flashing eyes of a panther. He sprang out upon the sand and lay on his back, purring or gnawing a bone; his fur shone with silver lights in the moonlight. I caught up a knotted stick and awaited the coming fray with eagerness."*

446. года́ and го́ды are both used as the pl. of го́дъ.

447. слезы́ : gen. sing. after the negative verb; the pl. is слёзы, слёзъ.

450. плы́вшій : past participle of плыть. Both плыть and пла́вать mean 'to sail,' 'to swim,' and both are imperfectives; but the first is definite, and the second indefinite. The distinction may be illustrated thus : лѣсъ пла́ваетъ на водѣ́, 'wood floats on water'; but лѣсъ плывётъ на водѣ́, 'the timber is afloat on the water.' A similar pair of verbs is бѣжа́ть and бѣ́гать, for which see n. to l. 47.

451—4. о-заренá, по-крѣ́та, о-круженá are predicative forms of past participles passive of perfective verbs. It should be noted that few imperfective verbs form a past participle in the passive: e.g. there are no such forms as о-зáрянный, по-крывáтый, ог кружённый.

453. стѣнóй: i.e. the surrounding forest.

455. по ней, 'along it': comp. по горáмъ (l. 60).

456. двухъ огнéй is the gen. of два огнá́: see n. to l. 221.

457. про-мчáли-сь, 'rushed past.'

мчáть-ся, 'to rush,' makes мчу-сь, мчúшь-ся in the present tense, and мчáл-ся, мчáла-сь in the past.

458. какóй-то, 'some': he cannot yet identify it: see n. to l. 20.

459. вѣ́-скочилъ: вы- is always accented, when prefix in a perfective verb.

460. нá-вз-ничь, 'on its back': лежáть ничкóмъ (ог ницъ) is 'to lie with the face down' (l. 232).

Note that one says лёгъ на песóкъ but лежáлъ на пескѣ́.

461. тó былъ...гость: see n. to l. 349.

гость, 'inhabitant': perhaps used here for the sake of the rhyme. Such words as мостъ do not properly rhyme with кость, the final letter being different. See n. to l. 666.

463. визжáть is properly 'to squeak'; it is often used contemptuously of the female voice.

464. тó, 'at times': no second тó follows.

465. мотáя...хвостóмъ, 'waving his tail.' Russian uses the instr. in many phrases of this kind, e.g. онъ по-качáлъ головóй, 'he shook his head.'

466. на нёмъ, 'on him,' i.e. the panther (not, I think, the tail).

467. от-ливáла-сь серебрóмъ, 'was shot with silver.' A material so woven as to show different colours at different angles, or such a jewel as a diamond, is said от-ливáть or от-ливáть-ся. 'Shot silk' is шёлкъ съ от-ли́вомъ. The verb was used in its original sense in l. 373.

468. с-хвати́въ, 'having caught up': past gerund, from с-хвати́ть.

рога́тый, lit. 'with horns,' from рогъ, ро́га: a 'knotted' bough is meant.

470. за-жгло́-ся for за-жгло́-сь. The past tense of за-же́чь, 'to kindle,' is за-жёгъ, за-жгла́, etc.

472. ины́мъ путёмъ, 'by a different path,' of monastic peace, unlike the warlike habits of his tribe.

474. быть бы могъ, 'I might have been.'
The personal pronouns are sometimes inserted and sometimes omitted; in this poem they are generally inserted.

въ краю́: the accent shows that краю́ is loc.

475. не изъ послѣ́днихъ, 'not one of the last,' i.e. one of the best. Note that послѣ́дній has 'soft' endings.

XVII.

476—492. "*Soon scenting his enemy, he snarled, couched down, and charged. But I was too quick for him, and laid his broad forehead open with my trusty bough. He turned right over and the blood streamed from his wound. But he soon came on again, and we fought to the death.*"

477. по-чу́ялъ, 'scented.' Compare Púshkin, *Onégin*, vi, 35:

по-чу́я мёртваго, храпя́тъ
и бью́т-ся ко́ни—

(scenting the corpse, the horses snort and struggle).

вой must be distinguished from бой (l. 492), and the verb выть from быть.

479. нача́ть, like ста́ть, cannot be followed by a perfective infinitive.

481. в-сталъ на дыбы́, 'reared up on his hind-legs.' This noun is used in the sing. in the phrase, во́лосъ у него́ ды́бомъ всталъ, 'his hair stood on end.'

при-лёгъ: the prefix gives the sense of nearness to the ground: comp. l. 337 при-па́лъ къ волнѣ́.

483. мнѣ: грозѝть governs the dat.

485. вѣренъ, скоръ: the predicative forms of вѣрный and скóрый.

487. раз-сѣкъ: past tense of раз-сѣчь. The prefix denotes separation.

490. лилá, 'was flowing': imperfective.

491. волнóй, 'in a stream,' or 'like a stream': the instr. has either meaning.

XVIII.

493—521. "*As he hurled himself at me, I struck him in the throat with my weapon. Then we closed and fell to the ground together and continued the conflict there. I fought as fiercely as my antagonist, and yelled as loudly; I might have been a wild beast born in the woods myself, with no power to utter anything but the cries of an animal. At last his strength began to fail. His eyes flashed for the last time and then closed in death; he had died face to face with his foe.*"

493. ко мнѣ...на грудь, 'towards me, at the breast,' i.e. at my breast.

494. 'But I had time to insert into his throat....' у-спѣть (with imperfective у-спѣвáть) is followed here, and regularly, by a perfective infinitive: an action is likely to be completed if there is time to perform it.

во-ткнýть has в-тыкáть as its imperfective.

495. два рáза, 'twice': another example of the gen. sing. following два: see n. to l. 3.

496. за-вы́лъ, 'howled,' i.e. gave a howl; but 'the wolves howled all night' would be всю ночь вóлки вы́ли, with the imperfective verb.

497. изъ = 'with.'

498. с-плетя́-сь, 'locked together,' is a pres. gerund, from the perfective с-плестѝ-сь. As a rule, a pres. gerund is formed only from an imperfective.

499. крѣпче, 'more tightly' : comparative of крѣпко.

лвухъ друзей : gen. after the comparative : see n. to l. 223. The nom. of двухъ друзей is два друга.

500. рáзомъ, 'together' : the instr. of разъ (a time) has come to be used as an adverb.

502. и я, 'I too,' as well as the beast.

стрáшенъ: predicative form of стрáшный; золъ and дикъ below are predicative forms of злой and дикій

506. волкóвъ : волкъ, вóлка makes вóлки, волкóвъ in the pl.

507. пóлогомъ, 'canopy.' Beds were protected by a пóлогъ in Russia a hundred years ago ; but the custom seems to be extinct. It is mentioned as a safeguard, not only against mosquitos but even against rats.

508. словá людéй, 'the language of men.' люди is used as the plural of человѣкъ.

509. за-бы́лъ, 'I had forgotten': the past perfective here answers to our pluperfect.

511. съ дѣтства, 'from childhood.'

512. инóму, 'any other.'

513. The three infinitives governed by сталъ are all, according to the invariable rule, imperfectives.

514. мéдленнѣй: comparative of мéдленно.

515. въ послѣдній разъ, 'for the last time.'

517. блес-ну́-ли, 'flashed once': -ну- is the suffix of unity of action.

519. съ comes closely after лицóмъ къ лицу́.

торжеству́ющимъ : instr. sing. masc., pres. part. act. of торжествовáть, of which the present tense is торжеству́ю, -ву́ешь, etc.

521. слѣдуетъ, 'it is right': an impersonal use of слѣдовать, 'to follow.'

боéцъ is declined, бойц-á, бойц-у́, etc.

XIX.

522—532. "*The wounds left by the panther's claws are open still; churchyard mould will heal them soon. Regardless of them, I struggled on through the forest, but fortune was determined to mock my efforts.*"

523. коготь, когтя, m., 'claw,' makes когти, когтей in the pl.

524. ещё не, 'not yet': уже не, 'no longer' (l. 9).

524, 5. The two perfective verbs correspond to English perfects.

526. сырой is (I think) m. sing., agreeing with покровъ. The noun was probably chosen for its double meaning: (1) covering; (2) pall, or hearse-cloth. ихъ: acc. pl.

о-свѣжитъ, 'will refresh': за-живитъ, 'will heal': both verbs are perfectives, and therefore their present tense has a future meaning: see Appendix, § 4.

529. со-бравъ: past gerund, from со-брать: see l. 74.

530. по-брёлъ я, 'I dragged myself on.' The present tense of по-брести is по-бреду, -ёшь, etc., and the past tense по-брёлъ, по-брела, -о, -и.

XX.

533—577. "*I came to an end of the forest, as the third day dawned. There were signs that seemed familiar to me; yet at first I was unwilling to believe that I had retraced my steps and come back to my former place of captivity. Was this the end of the dream I had cherished so long? Must I die so young after one taste of freedom? But the convent bell rang out, and I could doubt no longer: all my life long that sound had shattered my visions of home and friends. I knew now that I should never set foot again on my native soil.*"

533. изъ лѣсу: the preposition robs лѣсу of its accent: so изъ дому, 'from the house'; за моремъ, 'beyond the sea,' and many similar phrases.

For the gen. in -y, see n. to l. 421. The accent distinguishes it at once from the loc. in -ў́.

534. про-снул-ся, 'awoke,' is reflexive; but у-снул, 'fell asleep,' is not.

хоровóдъ is properly an open-air dance of village girls; then it comes to mean 'a bevy,' 'a company' generally, but retains a suggestion of beauty and grace.

535. свѣтил: gen. pl. with zero ending, like словъ from слóво.

на-пу́т-ственныхъ: because they guide the sailor or night-traveller on his путь (way). The viaticum (or eucharist given to a dying person) is на-пу́т-ствіе.

537. за-говорил, 'began to speak': the song of birds is meant.

For this sense of the prefix за-, comp. за-пѣли (l. 275).

538. курить-ся, 'to send forth smoke': comp. l. 9.

гулъ is shown by с-нóва in l. 561 to be the sound of the convent bell, but it is so distant that it is a mere гулъ and not a звонъ, which it becomes in l. 560.

539. про-бѣжáлъ: the perfective is used, because the sound stopped immediately: про-бѣгáлъ would be used of a continuous sound.

For the meaning of про- as a prefix, see n. to l. 415.

540. Distinguish сѣлъ, 'took a seat,' from сидѣлъ, 'was sitting.'

в-слу́шивать-ся сталъ: cf. l. 342.

541. с-молкъ онъ, 'it was silent': смолкъ, смóлкла is the past tense of с-мóлкнуть.

543. мнѣ знакóмъ, '*was* familiar to me.'

For знáкомъ, see l. 40.

546. вернýл-ся, 'I had returned.' The monastery is his prison.

548. зá-мыселъ: a compound of мысль (thought) with hard endings and the accent thrown back: so ý-мыселъ with the same meaning: both compounds change the gender to masc.

ласка́лъ and the three following verbs are imperfectives: they describe a state which continued for many days.

551. Бо́жій свѣтъ, 'God's world': cf. l. 693: a constant epithet of свѣтъ, almost without meaning.

552. при = 'mid.'

дубра́въ: gen. pl. дубра́ва is properly 'an oak-forest,' from дубъ, 'an oak'; but it was used by a poetical convention for forest trees in general. It is so used in Púshkin's early poetry; and a good deal of convention of this kind was swept away by Lérmontov, who is not afraid to call a birch a birch, or any other tree by its name.

553. по-зна́въ: past gerund, from по-зна́ть.

по- here attenuates the meaning of the verb, 'having learnt for a short time.'

554. у-не́сть: another way of spelling у-нести́.

за собо́й, 'behind me.'

For себя́ referring to other persons than the 3rd, see n. to l. 116: по-кажи́ мнѣ свой язы́къ, 'show me your tongue.'

555. тоску́ по ро́динѣ: cf. l. 50.

свято́й seems rather a feeble epithet in so strong a poem.

556. надё́ждъ: gen. pl.

557. Note that ва́шей is used; твое́й would mean something different.

559. я ду́малъ, 'I was thinking,' at the moment the bell began.

560. ко́локола is the gen. sing., колокола́ the nom. pl., of ко́локолъ.

561. раз-да́л-ся, 'rang out': with вдругъ the perfective is natural, but with до́лго the imperfective раз-дава́л-ся would be right.

563. его́, 'it': the звонъ, not the ко́локолъ.

564. съ дѣ́тскихъ глазъ, 'from my childish eyes.' The reader will have noticed how often such words as 'my, thy, his,' etc. are omitted in Russian.

не разъ, 'many a time'; lit. 'not once': comp. l. 666. This

must be distinguished from ни ра́зу (gen.), 'not even once,' 'never.'

565. с-гоня́лъ, 'used to drive away': imperfective of repeated action.

566. про, 'about,' takes acc.: cf. l. 746.

As бли́жніе and родны́е (nouns here) are animate beings, their acc. pl. has the form of the gen. pl.; and this applies to коне́й (horses) below; but би́тва is inanimate, and therefore the acc. pl. is би́твы, the same as the nom. pl.

567. степе́й: gen. pl. of степь.

568. Note that the adjectives, as well as the nouns, take the form of the gen. pl.

570. всѣхъ, and not всѣ, is another instance of tho rule givon on l. 566. See also n. to l. 115.

по-бѣжда́лъ, 'used to conquer.'

572. вы-ходи́лъ, 'was coming out'; the perfective is вы́шелъ (l. 533).

574. желѣзомъ, 'with iron,' i.e. an iron bar.

576. что мнѣ...не про-ложи́ть, 'that I should not set': for this use of the inf., see n. to l. 164.

слѣда́: gen. in the negative sentence.

XXI.

578—601. *"I deserved to fail, because my strength and courage were not equal to my desire. My prison had left its mark on me: I was like a flower that languished within prison walls till some kind hand transplanted it to a garden of roses; but it was too late, and the flower was soon burnt up by the sun's fierce rays."*

580. плоха́го: pronounce *pla-háw-va.*

с-бро́сивъ, 'having thrown off': gerund of с-бро́сить.

582. на-йдётъ, 'will find'; but на-хо́дитъ, 'finds.'

кра́ткій = коро́ткій: see n. to l. 14.

583. предъ нимъ, 'in comparison with him.'

584. полна́: predicative: the verb to be supplied is была́ or possibly есть.

585. то́ is the subject; the verb есть is understood. For this form of sentence, see n. to l. 349.

588. оста́вила, 'had left': the perfective represents our pluperfect.

тако́въ, '*is* like that.'

цвѣто́къ, 'a flower': the pl. is цвѣты́, but the diminutive form is used for a single flower.

589. темни́чный: adj. formed from темни́ца, 'a prison,' lit. 'a dark place.'

вы́-росъ: the accented prefix shows the verb to be perfective: see n. to l. 39.

590. блѣ́денъ: predicative form of блѣ́дный: see l. 65.

плитъ: gen. pl.

591. ли́стьевъ: gen., because the object of a negatived verb.

592. рас-пуска́лъ: the prefix denotes the expansion of the opening leaves. Here again the imperfective, rather than the perfective рас-пусти́лъ, accompanies до́лго.

всё, 'always': adv.

лучѣ́й: жда́ть and other verbs ' of expecting' are usually followed by the gen.

For the termination of луч-ѣ́й, see note to l. 205.

594. про-шло́, 'passed by': for the meaning of про-, see n. to l. 415. Distinguish between при-шла́ пора́, 'the time has come,' and про-шла́ пора́, ' the time has passed.'

про-шло́, neut. sing., agrees with мно́го, though мно́го is plur. in sense. This is the usual Russian idiom with numbers, even when the subject to the verb is neither neuter nor singular; e.g. про-шло́ два го́да, 'two years passed'; про-би́ло три часа́, 'it struck three.'

до́брая, 'kind.'

595. тро́нула-сь = была́ тро́нута.

596. пере-несёнъ: the prefix has the same force as 'trans-' in 'transfer': it signifies a change of place: cf. l. 725.

597. розъ: gen. pl.

598. бытіѧ́ = 'of God's world': the book of Genesis is кни́га Бытіѧ́.

599. что жъ, 'what came of it?': i.e. it was useless.

вз-о-шла́, 'had risen up.'

600. палѧ́щій: pres. participle of пали́ть.

об-жёгъ (also spelt об-жёгъ); fem. об-о-жгла́: past tense of об-же́чь, which has об-жига́ть for imperfective.

XXII.

602—629. "*So I too was burnt by the sun's pitiless rays. In vain I tried to bury my head in the scorched herbage: the earth itself was burning hot; the air quivered and the cliffs steamed with heat. No sound of running water or living creature broke the terrible silence, except a snake that rustled through the dry grass and glided over the sand, till even he hid from the burning sun.*"

602. его́, 'it,' i.e. the flower.

604. въ траву́, lit. 'into the grass,' прѧ́талъ being treated as if it were = в-со́вывалъ, 'I thrust in.'

605. главу́ = го́лову: see n. to l. 14.

606. из-со́хшій, 'dried up': past participle of из-со́хнуть.

вѣнцо́мъ терно́вымъ, 'like a crown of thorns': for this use of the instr., see n. to l. 127.

608. с-вива́л-ся: the simple imperfective, вил-сѧ́, would not convey the idea that the grasses twined *together*; hence the prefix с- is added; but с-вил-сѧ́ is perfective; so the compound imperfective is used.

огнёмъ дыша́ла, 'breathed fire,' in our idiom.

610. въ вышинѣ́: i.e. in the sky above me.

612. міръ Бо́жій: cf. Бо́жій свѣ́тъ (l. 551).

614. сномъ (which is to be taken with спалъ above) governs от-чаѧ́нья. 'To sleep the sleep of innocence' is спать сномъ неви́нности.

615. 'If only a corn-crake had called!' That would have been something, to break the silence. For хотя́, see n. to l. 120.

617. ручья́: gen. of ручéй.

618. ребя́чій: similarly we might describe a stream as 'babbling' or 'prattling.'

619. бурья́номъ: "the Russians call бурья́нъ all the herbaceous field plants." Boyer, p. 67.

шелестá: pres. gerund, from шелестѝть.

шéлестъ means much the same as шóрохъ (l. 371)—a dry rustling sound such as is produced by paper or withered leaves: мышь шелестѝтъ бумáгами на столѣ̀, 'a mouse is making the papers on the table rustle.'

621. златóй = золотóй (l. 664): see n. to l. 14.

622. дó-низу: до- is apt to keep the accent in adverbs thus formed: e.g. дó-сыта, 'to satiety.' дó-низу = 'all its length.'

623. браздя́ = борозд-я́: gerund of бороздѝть: comp. браздá (l. 327).

625. нѣжа-ся for нѣжа-сь: see n. to l. 2.

на нёмъ, 'on it,' i.e. the sand.

626. тройнѝмъ кольцóмъ, 'in a triple ring.' Cf. Lérmontov, *Demon*, Part II (of a snake):

> тó вдругъ совьётся въ три кольцá,
> тó ля́жетъ длѝнной полосóю,
> и блéщетъ какъ булáтный мечъ

(at one time it coils into three rings, at another it lies at length and flashes like a steel blade).

627. об-о-жженá: predicative form of об-о-жжёная, past participle pass. of об-жéчь.

629. пря́тала-сь: one would expect the perfective to mark the disappearance of the snake; but the imperfective, as the descriptive aspect, is retained to the end: see n. to l. 200.

XXIII.

630—695. *"Through the clear air I could descry the convent walls, beneath which the two rivers flowed, so far from my reach. I could neither stand nor speak, and delirium came over me. I dreamed that I was lying at the bottom of a river, with ice-cold water pouring down my parched throat, and I felt perfectly happy. The sun shone with a tempered heat through the mirror of the waters, and the fish swam over my head. One golden fish sang to me in a little silvery voice, and begged me to rest for ever in the cool river bed, and confessed her love for me. The voice of the fish and the ripple of the water seemed to blend in one. Then I became unconscious."*

631. свѣтло́, ти́хо: predicative forms of свѣтлое and ти́хое the first changes the accent, the second keeps it as before. No rule can be laid down.

пары́: acc. pl.

632. чернѣ́ли, 'showed black.' The verb is plural, but it must be remembered that горы́ is gen. sing.; the nom. pl. is го́ры.

633. одно́й, i.e. горы́.

634. зубча́тою: see l. 434.

635. в-низу́ is so accented because низу́ is loc., governed by въ. But с-ни́зу (from below) is accented on the first syll., because ни́зу is genitive.

636. об-ви́въ, lit. 'having surrounded'; past gerund: but our idiom is to use the present participle.

637. свѣ́жихъ: the 'freshness' of the islands is due to the rivers.

638. ше́пчущихъ: gen. pl. m., pres. part. of шепта́ть, of which the pres. tense is шепчу́, ше́пчешь, etc.

639. дру́жно, 'busily': or perhaps 'in amity': the rivers were compared to sisters in l. 3.

640. до = to reach, to get as far as.

642. за-кружи́ло-сь, 'began to go round.' For this sense of за-, see l 537.

644. без-зву́чный and не-дви́жимый are the longer forms.

645. я у-ми ра́лъ, 'I was fainting': у-мира́ть is often used to denote something less than actual death.

647. что я лежу́, 'that I was lying.' This retention of the present sequence in reported thought or speech is a regular characteristic of Russian idiom: 'I said that I would try,' я сказа́лъ что по-стара́ю-сь; ' you said that you loved him,' вы сказа́ли что вы лю́бите его́: in such cases the past tense must not be used.

648. ре́чки: a diminutive of ре́ка́, with the accent thrown back: so ру́чка from рука́.

650. ве́чную, properly 'unending,' has here the sense of 'intense.'

по-я́: pres. gerund, from пои́ть, 'to make drink,' a causal verb connected with пить, 'to drink.'

651. лёдъ: pronounce *lyot*.

652. журч-а́: pres. gerund, from журча́ть.

654. сла́дко (pronounce *slátka*) is the predicative form of a neuter adj.; лю́бо is an adverb.

658. сла́достне́й: for the accent on the comparative, see n. to l. 222, and comp. l. 662.

луны́, 'than the moon.'

659. ры́бокъ: gen. pl. of the diminutive ры́бка: ры́ба itself has рыбъ for gen. pl.

пёстрыя, 'motley,' refers to the different colours and markings of the fish.

стада́: but the sing. is ста́до.

662. други́хъ, 'than the rest.'

663. ко мнѣ ласка́ла-сь, 'made love to me.' The simple verb, ласка́ть, 'to caress,' takes an acc. as its direct object.

665. вила́-сь, ' swam '; but the word also conveys the waving motion of a fish's body in the water: see n. to l. 293.

666. не разъ, 'many times': see n. to l. 564.

разъ here rhymes to вилá-сь: this is very exceptional; a word ending in -ь is regarded as not rhyming to a word ending in -ъ. But глазъ is a true rhyme to разъ.

669. на-дивить-ся, 'to wonder enough,' = у-дивить-ся в-дóволь, 'to wonder your fill.'

This sense of the prefix на- is well seen in the pretty word, не-на-глядный : дитя моё не-на-глядное, 'my child, at whom I can never look long enough!'—a common expression of affection.

672. за-молкáлъ: imperfective, because it stopped more than once and began again.

673. онъ, 'it,' i.e. the voice.

674. о-стáнь-ся, pl. остáнь-те-сь: imperative of о-стáть-ся, 'to remain.'

675. при-вóльное seems to differ from вóльное by adding the idea of space to that of freedom.

The verb 'there is' must be supplied.

677. я со-зовý, 'I shall call together.'

Note (1) зовý (from звать), 'I call'; (2) по-зовý, 'I shall call'; (3) со-зовý, 'I shall call together.' The two latter verbs are both perfectives, so that their presents have a future sense. But observe that, whereas по- loses its meaning in the compound, со- retains it. See Appendix, §§ 5, 6.

мойхъ сестéръ: acc. pl. : свойхъ might have been used with the same meaning.

679. раз-веселймъ, 'shall cheer up': perfective: but веселймъ, imperfective, 'we are cheering up.'

тумáнный взоръ, 'thy lustreless eyes.'

681. у-снй: imperative of у-снýть.

по-стéль, 'the thing spread,' is properly the bedding, exactly the Latin *stratum*.

мягкá: the predicative form of мягкая : as we have seen, these forms very often, in the fem., accent the final syllable.

682. The по-крóвъ is the transparent water overhead.

683. про-йдýтъ, 'shall pass by.'

684. подъ, 'to the sound of,' 'accompanied by,' takes the acc. as here.

Note the different accent in го́воръ and раз-гово́ръ, ' conversation ' (l. 269).

685. не у-таю́, 'I shall not hide,' у-таи́ть being a perfective. For the imperfective, see l. 281.

In this stanza, the syllable -ю occurs ten times and bears the accent six times. To our ears the repetition is excessive; but Russian taste seems not to object: Púshkin has such lines as

гдѣ дни мои́ текли́ въ глуши́

(where my days flowed by in retirement), and

у-дивлена́, о-скорблена́,

едва́ дыша́, в-стаётъ она́

(surprised, insulted, hardly breathing, she gets up).

But they are not common.

690. мни́ло-сь, 'methought': impersonal form of a verb now obsolete, мнить, 'to think,' from which по́-мнить, 'to remember,' is formed. The noun мнѣ́ніе, 'opinion,' is still in common use.

693. тутъ, 'at that point.'

я за-бы́л-ся, 'I became unconscious': 'to come to' from a faint is о-по́мнить-ся, lit. 'to remember oneself.'

Бо́жій свѣтъ: see l. 551.

694. у-га́съ: the past tense of у-га́снуть is у-га́съ, у-га́сла, у-га́сло.

695. без-си́лью: dat., governed by the verb.

XXIV.

696—706. "*I was found unconscious and carried back here. That is the end of my story. I have but one regret, that my body will not lie in my native soil, and that the tale of my sufferings will die within these walls and call forth no regret for my fate.*"

696. Predicative forms of the participles на-йдённый and по́д-нятый.

697. остальнóе, 'the rest.'

698. кóнчилъ, 'have finished': the past perfective here answers to our perfect.

вѣрь: imperative of вѣрить which governs the dat.

702. тлѣть: imperfective: бýду is never followed by a perfective infinitive : see Appendix, § 9.

703—6. This regret is distinct from the other and seems out of character with the speaker.

704. не при-зовётъ, 'will not attract': for the perfective, see n. to со-зовý (l. 677).

705. вниманье: acc., although the verb which governs it is negatived : see n. to l. 243.

ни чьё, 'of anyone.'

706. на, 'lo.'

тёмное, 'obscure.'

XXV.

707—722. "*Give me your hand in sign of farewell. You feel how hot mine is—that fire has fed on my vitals from my youth up and has now consumed me. Even though my spirit should find rest in heaven, I would be glad to sacrifice immortality for a few minutes of life in the mountains where I was born.*"

707. прощáй, and the perfective простú, both mean 'forgive!,' but are also used for 'good-bye!' When the dying peasant says простú!—the former meaning is uppermost, and the proper answer is, Бóгъ тебя простúтъ, 'God will pardon you'; i.e. I am a sinner like yourself and have no grievance against you.

But the present speaker is entirely self-righteous, and means no more than 'good-bye!'

'To say good-bye' is прощáть-ся (простúть-ся).

рýку: acc. of рукá, with shift of accent.

708. моá, i.e. рукá.

въ огнѣ, 'is burning': so онъ въ кровú, 'he is bleeding.'

710. та́йс-я : for та́й-сь, gerund of та́йть-ся: see n. to с-лива́яс-я (l. 2).

711. пи́щи нѣтъ, 'there is no food,' the negative of пи́ща есть: see n. to l. 250.

712. онъ про-жёгъ, 'it has burnt through'; but про-жига́етъ, 'it is burning through.'

The 'prison' is his breast.

713. воз-вратя́т-ся, 'will return'; but воз-враща́ет-ся, 'is returning.'

714. кто may be used for кото́рый, when тотъ is the antecedent.

всѣмъ: dat. pl.

716. что мнѣ въ томъ, 'what is there to me in that,' i.e. 'what is that to me?'

пуска́й...мой духъ на-йдётъ, 'let my spirit find,' i.e. even supposing that it finds... For the construction, see n. to l. 144.

раю́ and краю́ are both locatives, as the accent shows.

717. за-о́блачномъ, 'beyond the clouds': so за грани́цу, 'abroad,' lit. 'beyond the frontier.'

719. за, 'for.'

нѣсколько, like мно́го and many other adverbs of number, governs the genitive.

722. я бъ...про-мѣня́лъ, 'I would exchange': cf. l. 87.

XXVI.

723—748. "*I must soon die. When the time comes, have me carried into the garden to the place where two white acacias grow. From there the Caucasus is visible; and the mountain breeze will perhaps breathe a last greeting to me. With the feeling that I have a friend near me, I shall be able to die at peace with mankind.*"

723. ста́ну у-мира́ть, 'shall come to die.'

ста́ну, like бу́ду, is used with imperfective infinitives to form a future: see Appendix, § 9.

724. тебѣ не дóлго ждать, 'you will not have long to wait': for this use of the inf., see n. to l. 164.

725. пере-нéсть: English uses the passive here, 'to be carried across': for the prefix пере-, see n. to l. 596.

велѝ: imperative of велѣть: the plur. of the past tense of вестѝ has exactly the same form: see l. 285.

726. тó, 'that,' not 'the.'

цвѣлѝ, 'used to bloom': 3rd plur., past tense of цвѣстѝ.

727. акáцій: gen. plur.: not to be confused with акáціи, gen. sing., which has four syllables, not three.

два кустá: see n. to двѣ сестрѝ (l. 3).

728. такъ густá, '*is* so thick': for the use of такъ with adjectives, see n. to l. 314.

729. The l. illustrates the convenience, or rather necessity, of the double form of the adjective in a language which omits the verb *to be*: свѣжій, being a long form, is seen at once to be an epithet of the noun, while душѝстъ, being a short form, is the predicate. Comp. l. 332.

731. игрáющій: pres. participle of игрáть.

листъ, 'foliage.'

732. по-ложѝть, 'to lay,' is the perfective of класть, while ложѝть-ся is itself the imperfective of лечь, 'to lie down.'

734. у-пью-ся, 'I shall intoxicate myself': a perfective compound of пить, 'to drink': the corresponding imperfective is у-пивáю-сь. For the termination, see n. to l. 2.

въ послѣдній разъ: see l. 515.

735. вѝденъ: predicative form of вѝдный.

736. съ, 'from,' coalesces wholly with the following word.

737. при-шлётъ, 'will send,' from при-слáть: the imperfective, при-сылáетъ = 'is sending.'

740. роднóй...звукъ, 'the dear native sound' of the mountain breeze: the adj. implies both ideas.

раз-дáст-ся, 'will be heard,' lit. 'will spread itself': the imperfective, раз-даёт-ся = 'is being heard.'

742. с-клонѝвши-сь: past gerund, from с-клонѝть-ся.

743. о-тёръ, 'has wiped away': past tense of о-теréть, with fem. о-тёрла.

All compounds of терéть are perfective, all of тирáть are imperfective.

744. съ лицá, 'from my face.'

кончúны: gen. governed by потъ.

хлáдный = холóдный: see n. to l. 14.

745. въ-пол-гóлоса, lit. 'in half a voice': гóлоса is gen., governed by пол-.

747. я за-снý, ' I shall go to sleep': the imperfective, я за-сыпáю-сь, 'I am going to sleep,' is reflexive in form.

748. про-клянý, 'shall curse.'

про-клясть makes про-клянý, -ёшь, etc.: the imperfective, про-клинáть, makes про-клинáю. The boy means that this farewell greeting from his native mountains enables him, in spite of the wrongs he has suffered, to die at peace with all the world.

APPENDIX

ASPECTS—IMPERFECTIVE AND PERFECTIVE.

1.   Every verbal notion may be expressed in Russian in either of two Aspects, the Imperfective and Perfective; and every Russian verb belongs to one or other of these two Aspects.

2.   Most perfective verbs are compound, being formed by the addition of a prefix (such as по-, на-, воз-, вы-, and others) to a simple and imperfective verb: thus писа́ть (*to write*) is imperfective, but на-писа́ть (*to write*) is perfective[1].

3.   A verb in the imperfective aspect expresses continued or repeated action:

> я писа́лъ весь день,
> *I was writing all day.*

A verb in the perfective aspect expresses completed action:

> вчера́ я на-писа́лъ къ вамъ,
> *I wrote to you yesterday.*

4.   The present tense of every imperfective is present in meaning: e.g.

> я пишу́,
> *I write*, or, *I am writing.*

But the present tense of every perfective is future in meaning:

> я на-пишу́,
> *I shall write.*

5.   Any prefix which serves merely to convert an imperfective verb into a perfective loses its special meaning.

Thus на-, when used as a prefix, generally bears the meaning of *on* or *against*; but я на-пишу́ means simply, *I shall write.*

6.   Any other prefix than на-, placed before -писа́ть, retains its meaning: hence о-писа́ть = *to describe*, пере-писа́ть = *to copy*, под-писа́ть = *to sign*, etc.

7.   Those prefixes which retain their meaning also change the imperfective verb, e.g. писа́ть, to a perfective.

Hence я о-пишу́ means *I shall describe.*

8.   How then is it possible to express *I am describing*?

This is done by a change in the stem of the verb[2].

Either -ив- or -ыв- is inserted between the stem and

---

[1]   писа́ть = γράφειν, and на-писа́ть = γράψαι: the perfective is in fact an 'aorist voice.'

[2]   Comp. the change by which βάλλειν, when compounded with any other element than a preposition, becomes -βολεῖν.

termination of the simple verb; and every compound of this form is imperfective, and the prefixes keep their meaning: e.g.

о-пи́с-ыв-аю, *I describe,*
пере-пи́с-ыв-аю, *I copy,*
под-пис-ыв-аю, *I sign.*

9.　It has been explained already that the perfective has no true present.　Similarly, the imperfective has no true future, but makes one with an auxiliary verb, as English does:

бу́ду писа́ть, *I shall write* (not once, but from time to time).

N.B.　Auxiliary verbs, such as бу́ду, ста́ну, пере-ста́ну, etc., are never followed by a perfective infinitive.

10.　Both aspects form an imperative:

(i)　пиши́, пиши́те;
(ii)　на-пиши́, на-пиши́те.

Of these, the perfective imperative, на-пиши́, is the more peremptory.

11.　Both aspects form a past tense:

(i)　я писа́лъ, *I was writing, I used to write, I tried to write.*

N.B.　This aspect is commonly used in negative and interrogative sentences, even where the sense of 'continuance' is not obvious.

(ii)　я на-писа́лъ, *I wrote, I have written, I had written.*

12.　Both aspects form past participles, active and passive, and a past gerund:

(i)　писа́вшій, пи́санный, писа́въ,
(ii)　на-писа́вшій, на-пи́санный, на-писа́въ.

13.　But the pres. participles and pres. gerund,

пи́шущій, писа́емый and пиша́,

are formed only from the imperfective aspect.

14.　In every part of the verb which is found in both aspects, completed action is expressed by the perfective, and continuous action by the imperfective.　The distinction is generally clear enough; but, in the case of the past tense and the infinitive, it is difficult at times to account for the aspect chosen.

Note.　Much fuller information will be found in Forbes' *Russian Grammar,* §§ 101—117; see also Boyer's *Russian Reader,* the Index under the heading *Aspect.*

VOCABULARY

Most of the abbreviations will be readily understood : *instr.* stands for the instrumental case, and *loc.* for the locative or prepositional.

The gender of nouns is given only where the termination of the nominative leaves the gender doubtful.

Where two infinitive forms of the verb are given together, the first is always imperfective, the second, in brackets, perfective.

The order of the alphabet is : а, б, в, г, д, е, ж, з, и, і, й, к, л, м, н, о, п, р, с, т, у, ф, х, ц, ч, ш, щ, ъ, ы, ь, ѣ, э, ю, я. Of these, й, ъ, ы, ь, are never initial.

а, *but, and.*
азъ, *I* (archaic).
акація, *acacia.*
алмазъ, —а, *diamond.*
алтарь, —ря, m., *altar.*
áнгелъ, —а, *angel.*
Арáгва, *the Aragva.*
аýлъ, —а, *village.*

барсъ, —а, *panther.*
бахромá, *a fringe.*
бáшня, —и, *tower.*
бéз-дна, *abyss.*
без-жáлостный, *pitiless.*
без-звýчный, *soundless.*
без-мóлвный, *speechless.*
без-полéзно, adv., *uselessly.*
без-силіе, *weakness.*

без-сильный, *powerless.*
без-ýмный, *senseless.*
безъ, prep. with gen., *without.*
безъискýсственно, adv., *artlessly.*
бéрегъ, *bank.*
бéрежно, adv., *warily.*
бúтва, *combat.*
бить (по-бúть), *to beat.*
благо-вóнный, *fragrant.*
благо-дарúть (по-благо-дарúть), *to thank.*
благо-дáть, —и, f., *blessing.*
блажéнный, *blissful.*
блажéнство, *bliss.*
блескъ, —а, *glitter.*
блестѣть (блеснýть), *to glitter.*

бли́же, adv., *nearer*.

бли́жнiе, *relations*.

бли́зкiй, *near*.

близъ, prep. with gen., *near*.

блѣ́дный, *pale*.

боево́й, —а́я, —о́е, *martial*.

бое́цъ, бойца́, *a fighter*.

Бо́жiй, —жья, —жье, *of God, divine*.

бой, бо́я, *a fight, battle*.

больно́й, —о́го, *sick*; noun, *the invalid, patient*.

бо́льше (and бо́лѣе), adv., *further*.

болѣ́знь, —и, f., *illness, disease*.

борьба́, *a struggle*.

боязли́вый, *frightened*.

боя́ться (по-боя́ться), *to fear*.

бразда́, *a furrow*.

бразди́ть, *to furrow*.

братъ, *brother*; pl. бра́тья, —ьевъ.

бредъ, *delirium*.

брести́ (по-брести́), *to drag oneself along*.

броди́ть (по-броди́ть), *to wander*.

бу́детъ : see быть.

бу́дто (and бу́дто бы), adv., *as it were, as if, like*.

бу́рный, *stormy*.

бурья́нъ, —а, *herbage*.

бу́ря, *a storm*.

бы (or бъ) : conditional particle.

былъ, была́, бы́ло : past tense of быть.

бы́стро, adv., *quickly*.

быстрота́, *speed*.

бытiе́, —iя́, *existence*.

быть, *to be*; fut. бу́ду, —ешь; imperative будь; быть мо́жетъ, *may-be, perhaps*.

бѣ́гать (по-бѣ́гать), *to run (often)*.

бѣгъ, —a, *course*.

бѣ́дный, *poor*.

бѣжа́ть (по-бѣжа́ть), *to run, speed on*.

бѣ́лый, *white*.

бѣ́шенство, *fury*.

бѣ́шеный, *furious*.

ва́жность, —и, f., *dignity*.

валъ, —a, *a wave*.

вамъ : dat. of вы.

васъ : gen., acc., loc. of вы.

вашъ, ва́ша, ва́ше, *yours*.

в-верху́, adv., *aloft*.

в-дали́, adv., *in the distance*.

вдругъ, adv., *suddenly*.

в-дыха́ть (в-дохну́ть), *to breathe in*.

везти́ (по-везти́), *to convey*.

велѣ́ть, *to command*.

вертѣ́ть (верну́ть), *to turn*; верну́ться, *to return*.

верши́на, *summit*.

ве́село, adv., *gleefully*.

весёлый, *cheerful, joyful*.

вести (по-вести), *to lead, carry on.*

весь, вся, всё, *all.*

вечерній, adj., *evening.*

вечеръ, *evening* ; pl. вечера.

в-замѣнъ, prep. with gen., *in exchange for.*

вз-глядъ, —а, *a look.*

вз-глядывать (вз-глянуть), *to look.*

вз-дыхать (вз-дохнуть), *to sigh.*

вз-о-йти (вс-ходить), *to ascend*, past tense вз-о-шёлъ.

взоръ, —а, *a look.*

видный, *visible.*

видъ, —а, *aspect, sight.*

видѣніе, *a vision.*

видѣть (у-видѣть), *to see.*

визжать (за-визжать), *to yell.*

виноградный, adj., *of a vine.*

висѣть (по-виснуть), *to hang* (intr.).

виться (с-виться), *to twine* (intr.), *rise up, move.*

в-кушать (в-кусить), *to taste.*

влажный, *moist.*

власть, —и, f., *power.*

в-ливаться (в-литься), *to flow into.*

в-лѣзать (в-лѣзть), *to climb up.*

в-мѣстѣ, adv., *together.*

в-низу, adv., *beneath.*

в-низъ, adv., *downward.*

в-ниманіе, *attention.*

в-нимательный, *attentive.*

в-новь, adv., *anew, again.*

в-нятный, *intelligible.*

во = въ.

вода, *water.*

воз-вращаться (воз-вратить-ся), *to return.*

воз-духъ, *air.*

вой, воя, *a yell, howl.*

волкъ, —а, *wolf.*

волна, *a wave.*

волшебный, *magical.*

вольность, —и, f., *freedom.*

вольный, *free.*

воля, *freedom.*

ворота, воротъ (pl. only), *entrance gate.*

вос-питывать (вос-питать), *to bring up.*

вос-по-минаніе, *recollection.*

востокъ, —а, *the East.*

во-ткнуть : see в-тыкать.

вотъ, *lo ! see !*

врагъ, —а, *an enemy.*

в-ручать (в-ручить), *to hand over.*

всё, adv., *always, all the time.*

вс-кормить, *to feed up.*

в-слушиваться (в-слушать), *to listen.*

вс-помнить : see помнить.

в-ставать (в-стать), *to stand up.*

встрѣча, *a meeting.*

встрѣча́ть (встрѣ́тить), *to meet.*

вс-ходи́ть (вз-о-йти́), *to rise.*

всѣ : pl. of весь.

всѣхъ : gen. and loc. pl. of весь.

в-тыка́ть (во-ткну́ть), *to thrust in.*

въ (and во), prep. with acc. or loc., *at (of time), in, into, to, on.*

въ-пол-го́лоса, *in a low voice.*

вы : plural of ты.

вы-лета́ть (вы́-летѣть), *to fly out.*

вы-раста́ть (вы́-рости), *to grow up.*

вы-рыва́ть (вы́-рвать), *to tear out.*

вы-ска́кивать (вы́-скочить), *to spring out.*

вы́-слушать, *to hear out.*

высо́кій, *high.*

высота́, *height.*

высь, —и, f., *height.*

выть (за-вы́ть), *to howl.*

вы-ходи́ть (вы́-йти), *to come out, go out* ; вы́-шелъ, past tense of вы́-йти.

вы́-шелъ : see вы-ходи́ть.

вышина́, *height.*

вѣкъ, —а, *a century.*

вѣне́цъ, —нца́, *crown, wreath.*

вѣрить (по-вѣ́рить), *to believe.*

вѣ́рный, *true.*

вѣтвь, —и, f., *branch.*

вѣтеро́къ, —рка́, *a breeze.*

вѣ́теръ, —тра, *a wind.*

вѣ́чность, —и, f., *eternity.*

вѣ́чный, *eternal.*

вѣ́ять (по-вѣ́ять), *to be wafted.*

вя́нуть (за-вя́нуть), *to fade.*

га́снуть (по-га́снуть), *to go out (of fire).*

гдѣ, adv., *where.*

генера́лъ, —а, *a general.*

ги́бкій, *bending, pliant.*

ги́бнуть (по-ги́бнуть), *to perish.*

глава́ = голова́.

гла́дкій, *smooth.*

глазъ, —а, *eye* ; pl. глаза́.

гласъ = го́лосъ.

глубина́, *depth.*

глубо́кій, *deep.*

глубо́ко, adv., *deep.*

глухо́й, —а́я, —о́е, *dull, deaf.*

говори́ть (сказа́ть), *to speak, to say.*

го́воръ, *speech, sound.*

годъ, —а, *year* ; pl. го́ды and года́.

голова́, *head.*

го́лодъ, *hunger.*

голосо́къ, —ска́, *little voice.*

го́лосъ, *voice* ; pl. голоса́.

голубо́й, —а́я, —о́е, *blue.*

го́лубь, —я, m., *pigeon.*

гора́, *mountain.*
го́рдо, *proudly.*
го́рдый, *proud.*
го́рло, *throat.*
го́рный, adj., *of the mountains.*
го́рькій, *bitter.*
горѣ́ть (с-горѣ́ть), *to burn* (intr.).
горя́чій, *burning, hot.*
гость, —я, m., *guest, visitor.*
грань, —и, f., *boundary, fence.*
гроза́, *thunder-storm.*
гроздъ, *bunch, cluster.*
грози́ть, *to threaten.*
гро́зно, adv., *menacingly.*
гро́мко, adv., *loudly.*
гру́да, *a heap.*
грудь, —и, f., *breast.*
Грузи́нка, *a Georgian woman.*
Гру́зія, *Georgia.*
гру́сто-нѣ́жный, *sadly tender.*
грызть (грызну́ть), *to gnaw.*
губа́, *lip.*
гудѣ́ть (за-гудѣ́ть), *to roar.*
гулъ, *noise.*
густо́й, —а́я, —о́е, *thick.*
гу́ще : comparative of густо́й.

да, *yes ; but, and.*
дава́ть (дать), *to give.*
давно́, adv., *long ago.*
давны́мъ-давно́, *long ago.*
да́-же, *even.*
далёкій, *distant.*
далеко́, adv., *far away.*

да́льный, *distant.*
дань, дана́, дано́, *given.*
дать : see дава́ть.
два, двѣ̀, два, *two.*
дверь, —и, f., *door.*
двухъ : gen. of два.
двѣ̀ : fem. of два.
день, дня, m., *day.*
де́рево, — а, n., *tree* ; pl. дерева́, дерёвъ.
держа́ть (по-держа́ть), *to hold* ; держа́ться, *to hold on.*
ди́кій, *wild.*
дитя́, —тя́ти, *child* ; n. pl. дѣ́ти.
дли́нный, *long.*
для, prep. with gen., *for, for the sake of.*
дней : gen. pl. of день.
днёмъ : instr. of день.
дни : pl. of день.
дно, дна, *bottom.*
дню : dat. of день.
дня : gen. of день.
до, prep. with gen., *as far as.*
до́брый, *kind.*
добы́ча, *prey, booty.*
дождь, —дя́, m., *rain.*
до́лгій, *long.*
до́лго, adv., *at length, for long.*
доли́на, *valley.*
домо́й, adv., *homewards.*
домъ, —а, *house, home.*
до́-низу, adv., *to the tip.*
до-про́съ, —а, *questioning.*

доро́га, *way, path*.
дорого́й, *precious, costly*.
дохну́ли: see дыха́ть.
друго́й, —а́я, —о́е, *other, second*.
друг, —а, *friend*; pl. друзья́, друзе́й.
дру́жба, *friendship*.
дру́жескiй, *friendly*.
дру́жно, adv., *stoutly*.
дру́жный, *sociable*.
дубра́ва, *oak-forest*.
ду́ма, *thought*.
ду́мать (по-ду́мать), *to think*.
дух, —а, *spirit*.
душа́, *soul*.
души́стый, *fragrant*.
ду́шный, *stifling*.
дыба́, *a lever*; стать на дыбы́, *to rear up erect*.
дыми́ться, *to smoke*.
дымо́к, —мка́, *faint smoke*.
дым, —а, *smoke*.
дыха́ть (дохну́ть), *to breathe*.
дыша́ть (по-дыша́ть), *to breathe*.
де́лать (с-де́лать), *to do*.
де́ло, *thing, doing*.
де́тскiй, *childish*.
де́тство, *childhood*.

его́, *him, it*; acc. of он.
его́, *of him, his*; gen. of он.
едва́, adv., *barely*.
её: acc. of она́.

ему́: dat. of он.
е́сли, *if*.
есть, *there is*.
ещё, adv., *still*; ещё не, *not yet*.
е́ю (and ей): instr. of она́.
ей, *her*; gen. of она́.

жа́дно, adv., *thirstily*.
жа́дный, *thirsty, eager*.
жа́жда, *thirst*.
жа́ждать, *to thirst for*.
жа́лоба, *complaint*.
жа́лобный, *plaintive*.
жа́лость, —и, f., *pity*.
жаль, adv.; мне жаль, *I regret*.
жар, —а, *heat*.
ждать (подо-жда́ть), *to wait for*.
же (and ж), enclitic particle, *and, but*.
жела́нiе, *a wish*.
жела́ть (по-жела́ть), *to wish*.
жёлтый, *yellow*.
желе́зо, *an iron bar*.
жечь (с-жечь), *to burn* (tr.).
живи́тельный, *life-giving*.
жи́во, adv., *quickly*; живе́й, *more quickly*.
живо́й, *alive, lively*.
жизнь, —и, f., *life*.
жить (про-жи́ть), *to live*.
житьё, *life*.
жре́бiй, *fate*.

журча́ть, *to babble.*

за, prep. with acc. and instr., *behind, beyond, for, by.*

за-быва́ть (за-бы́ть), *to forget.*

за-бы́тый, *forgotten.*

за-вы́лъ : see выть.

за-говори́ть, *to begin to speak.*

за-ду́мывать (за-ду́мать), *to plan.*

за-живля́ть (за-живи́ть), *to heal (a wound).*

за зжига́ться (за-же́чься), *to take fire.*

за-кипѣ́лъ : see кипѣ́ть.

зако́нный, *fixed by law.*

за-кружи́ться, *to turn round.*

за-крыва́ть (за-кры́ть), *to cover over.*

за-лега́ть (за-ле́чь), *to penetrate, settle down.*

за-лётный, *migratory.*

за-молка́ть (за-мо́лкнуть), *to be silent.*

за́-мыселъ, —сла, *purpose.*

за-не-мога́ть (за-не-мо́чь), *to fall sick.*

за-ны́ть : see ныть.

за-о́блачный, *beyond the clouds.*

за-пѣва́ть (за-пѣ́ть), *to begin singing.*

за-раста́ть (за-рости́), *to heal* (intr.).

заря́, —и́, *dawn.*

за-слу́живать (за-служи́ть), *to deserve.*

за-сну́ть : see за-сыпа́ть.

за-стона́ть : see стона́ть.

за-сыпа́ть (за-сну́ть), *to fall asleep.*

за-творя́ть (за-твори́ть), *to shut.*

за-чѣ́мъ, *why ? what for ?*

звать (по-зва́ть), *to call.*

звонъ, —a, *ringing sound.*

звукъ, —a, *a sound.*

звуча́ть (про-звуча́ть), *to ring out.*

зву́чный, *sounding.*

звѣзда́, *a star* ; pl. звѣ́зды.

звѣрь, — я, m., *wild beast.*

здѣсь, adv., *here.*

зелёный, *green.*

зе́лень, —и, f., *verdure.*

земля́, —и́, *earth.*

злато́й = золото́й.

зло, зла, *evil.*

злой, зла́я, зло́е, *evil, cruel.*

змѣя́, *a snake.*

знако́мый, *familiar.*

знакъ, —a, *a sign.*

знать (у-зна́ть), *to know.*

зной, зно́я, *sultry heat.*

золоти́стый, *golden.*

зо́лото, —a, *gold.*

золото́й, —а́я, —о́е, *golden.*

золъ = злой.

зрачёкъ, —чка́, *pupil of the eye.*

зубе́цъ, —бца́, *tooth, point.*
зубча́тый, *toothed, serrated, battlemented.*

и, *and, even, also.*
игра́, *sport, play.*
игра́ть (с-ыгра́ть), *to play.*
идти́ (по-йти́), иду́, идёшь, *to come, go (on foot).*
из-ги́бъ, —а, *a fold.*
из-грыза́ть (из-гры́зть), *to devour.*
из-далека́, adv., *from far.*
из-му́ченный, *exhausted.*
из-мѣня́ть (из-мѣни́ть), *to betray.*
из-не-мога́ть (из-не-мо́чь), *to lose strength.*
из-нурённый, *exhausted.*
из-река́ть (из-ре́чь), *to pronounce.*
из-со́хшій, *dried, withered.*
из-ступле́ніе, *fury.*
изъ, prep. with gen., *from, from among.*
изъ-за, prep. with gen., *from behind.*
изъ-подъ, prep. with gen., *from under.*
и́ли (and иль), *or.*
имъ : instr. sing. and dat. plur. of онъ.
имѣ́ть (воз-ымѣ́ть), *to have, possess.*

и́мя, —ени, n., *name* ; pl. имена́, имёнъ.
иногда́, adv., *from time to time.*
ино́й, —а́я, —о́е, *different.*
и́нокъ, *a monk.*
и́скра, *a spark.*
иску́сство, *art.*
и́с-по-вѣдь, —и, f., *confession.*
ис-пу́ганный, *frightened.*
ис-пы́тывать (ис-пыта́ть), *to experience.*
исчеза́ть (исче́знуть), *to disappear.*
ихъ : acc. plur. of онъ, она́.
ихъ : gen. plur. of онъ, она́ : *of them, their.*

Кавка́зъ, *the Caucasus.*
кади́льница, *a censer.*
ка́ждый, *each.*
каза́ться, *to seem.*
кайма́, *a fringe.*
како́й-то, *of some kind.*
какъ, *how, when, as.*
какъ бу́дто, *as if, like.*
ка́менный, *stony, of stone.*
ка́мень, —мня, m., *a stone* ; pl. ка́мни, камне́й.
карава́нъ, —а, *a flock.*
каса́ться (косну́ться), *to touch.*
кати́ться (по-кати́ться), *to roll.*
ке́лья, ке́ли, *a cell* ; gen. pl. ке́лій.
кида́ть (ки́нуть), *to throw.*

кинжа́лъ, —а, *a dagger.*

кипѣ́ть (за-кипѣ́ть), *to boil, seethe, rage.*

класть (по-ложи́ть), *to lay, place.*

клинокъ, —нка́, *sword-blade.*

кля́сться (про-кля́сться), *to swear.*

кля́тва, *an oath.*

кни́га, *book.*

ко = къ.

когда́, *when* ; когда́ нибу́дь, *at some time.*

по́готь, ко́гти, *claw.*

ко́локолъ, *a bell.*

колыбе́ль, —и, f., *cradle.*

кольцо́, *a ring.*

кольчу́га, *coat of mail.*

коне́цъ, конца́, *end.*

коне́чно, *of course.*

конча́ть (ко́нчить), *to end.*

кончи́на, *death.*

конь, —я́, m., *steed, horse.*

ко́рень, —рня, m., *root* ; pl. ко́рни.

коросте́ль, —я́, m., *corncrake.*

кость, —и, f., *bone.*

кото́рый, —ая, —ое, *who, which.*

край, кра́я, *edge* ; *country.*

красова́ться, *to be beautiful.*

красота́, *beauty.*

кра́сться (у - кра́сться), *to glide, steal.*

кра́ткій, *brief, short.*

кри́кнуть: a perfective of крича́ть.

крикъ, —а, *cry.*

крича́ть (за-крича́ть), *to shout, cry.*

крова́вый, *bloody.*

кро́вля, *roof.*

кровь, —и, f., *blood.*

круговой, adj., *round.*

круго́мъ, adv., *around.*

круго́мъ, prep. with gen., *around.*

кружи́ться, *to be dizzy, to dance.*

крути́ться (за-крути́ться), *to eddy.*

круто́й, —а́я, —о́е, *steep.*

крыло́, *wing* ; pl. кры́лья.

крыльцо́, *balcony.*

крѣ́пче, adv., *more tightly.*

кто, *who, any.*

кто́-нибудь, *someone.*

кувши́нъ, —а, *pitcher.*

куда́, *whither ?*

ку́дри, —е́й, f. pl., *curls, tendrils.*

Кура́, *the Kurá.*

кури́ться (по-кури́ться), *to smoke.*

кустъ, —а́, *bush.*

къ (and ко), prep. with dat., *to, towards.*

кѣ́мъ-нибудь : instr. of кто́-нибудь.

лай, лáя, *barking.*

лáпа, *a paw.*

ласкáть(по-ласкáть),*to fondle, cherish.*

ласкáться, *to make love to.*

лáсково, adv., *playfully.*

лáсточка, *a swallow* ; gen. pl. лáсточекъ.

лёгкій, *light, easy, swift.*

легкó, adv., *lightly, easily.*

лёгъ, леглá, леглó : past tense of лечь : see ложúться.

лёдъ, льда, *ice.*

лежáть(по-лежáть),*to be lying.*

лéпетъ, *babbling.*

летáть, *to fly.*

ли (and ль) : interrogative particle.

листóкъ, —ткá, *leaflet.*

листъ, —á, *leaf, leafage* ; pl. лúстья, —ьевъ, and листы́.

лить (про-лúть), *to pour.*

лицó, *face.*

лишь, adv., *only.*

лобъ, лба, *forehead.*

ловúть (поймáть), *to catch.*

ложúться (лечь), *to lie down.*

лозá, *vine-branch.*

лунá, *the moon.*

лýнный, *moonlit.*

лýчше, *better.*

лучъ, —á, *ray.*

ль = ли.

лѣснóй, —áя, —óе, *of the forest.*

лѣсъ, —а, *forest.*

лѣтній, adj., *summer.*

лѣто, *summer.*

любúть (по-любúть), *to love.*

лю́бо, adv., *agreeably.*

любóвь, —бвú, f., *love.*

лю́ди, людéй, instr. людьмú, *people* ; used as pl. of человѣ́къ.

людскóй, —áя, —óе, *human.*

мáло, adv., *little* ; noun, *a little.*

мать, мáтери, f., *mother.*

мгла, *mist.*

мгновéнно, adv., *instantly.*

мéдленно, adv., *slowly.*

мéдленнѣй, *more slowly.*

мёдъ, —а, *honey.*

мéжду (and межъ), prep. with instr. or gen., *between.*

мелькáть (мелькнýть),*to flash.*

меня́ : acc. and gen. of я.

метáться (метнýться), *to writhe.*

мечтá, *a dream, fancy.*

мечтáніе, *a dream.*

мигъ, —а, *a moment.*

милліóнъ, —а, *a million.*

мúлый, *dear, beloved.*

минýта, *a minute.*

минýтный, *momentary.*

мúрный, *peaceful.*

міръ, —а, *world.*

мнúлось, impers., *methought.*

мно́го, adv., *many, much.*

мнѣ : dat. of я.

моги́ла, *a grave.*

моги́льный, *sepulchral.*

могу́чій, *strong, vigorous.*

могъ, могла́, могло́ : past tense of мочь.

мо́жно, *it is possible.*

мой, моя́, моё, *my* ; nom. plur. мои́.

моли́тва, *a prayer.*

моли́ть (по-моли́ть), *to pray.*

мо́лнія, *lightning.*

молодо́й, —а́я, —о́е, *young.*

мо́лча, adv., *in silence.*

молчали́вый, *silent.*

мольба́, *prayer.*

монасты́рь, —я́, m., *monastery.*

мона́хъ, *a monk.*

мона́шескій, *monastic.*

мота́ть (на-мота́ть), *to wave.*

мохъ, —а, *moss.*

мочь (с-мочь), *to be able.*

мракъ, *darkness.*

мра́чный, *gloomy.*

му́ка, *torment.*

мучи́тельный, *painful.*

мцы́ри, *a novice.*

мы : pl. of я.

мы́сленно, adv., *in thought.*

мысль, —и, f., *thought.*

мѣ́сто, *place.*

мѣ́сяцъ, —а, *the moon.*

мя́гкій, *soft.*

на, prep. with acc. or loc., *on, in, to, upon, for.*

на́-взничь, adv., *on its back.*

на-встрѣ́чу, adv., *to meet.*

на-вѣ́ки, adv., *for ever.*

на-вѣ́къ, adv., *for ever.*

наде́жда, *hope.*

надёжный, *trusty.*

на-диви́ться, *to wonder enough.*

на́д-пись, —и, f., *inscription.*

надъ (and на́до), prep. with instr., *over.*

на-за́дъ, adv., *backwards*

на-йдённый, *found* ; part. of на-йти́.

на-йдётъ : see на-ходи́ть.

на-коне́цъ, adv., *at last.*

на-правля́ть (на-пра́вить), *to direct.*

напра́сно, adv., *in vain.*

напра́сный, *vain.*

на-пу́тственный, *guiding.*

на-ро́дъ, —а, *people.*

на-ря́дъ, *apparel.*

на-става́ть (на-ста́ть), *to arrive.*

насъ : acc., gen., loc. of мы.

на-ходи́ть (на-йти́), *to come on, find.*

начина́ть (нача́ть), *to begin.*

на-шли́, *they found* : see на-ходи́ть.

нашъ, —а, —е, *our, ours.*

не, *not.*

небе́сный, adj., *of heaven.*

не́бо, *heaven, sky* ; pl. небеса́,
—е́съ.
не-во́льный, *involuntary.*
не-вѣ́домый, *unknown.*
не-глубо́кій, *not deep.*
не-далеко́, adv., *not far off.*
не-дви́жимый, *immoveable.*
не-дви́жный, *immoveable.*
неду́гъ, —а, *sickness.*
неё = её.
не-знако́мый, *unacquainted,
unknown.*
не-зри́мый, *unseen.*
не-зы́блемый, *immoveable.*
ней : loc. of она́.
не-ло́вкость, —и, fem., *awk-
wardness.*
не-мо́лчный, *incessant.*
нему́ = ему́.
нёмъ : loc. of онъ.
не-на-ви́дѣть (воз-не-на-ви́-
дѣть), *to hate.*
не-пре-кло́нный, *unbending.*
не-про-ница́емый, *impassable.*
не-я́сный, *unclear, dim.*
ни, negative particle, *not even* ;
neither, nor.
низ-ве́рженный, *hurled down.*
ни-когда́, *never.*
никому́ : dat. of никто́.
никто́, *no one* ; gen. and acc.
никого́.
нимъ = имъ.
нихъ = ихъ.
ницъ, adv., *face downwards.*

ни-чего́, *nothing.*
но, *but.*
нога́, *foot, leg.*
ножны́, —жёнъ, f. pl., *scabbard.*
ночле́гъ, —а, *couch.*
ночно́й, —а́я, —о́е, *of the
night.*
ночь, —и, f., *night.*
но́ша, *burden.*
нужда́, *need.*
ны́нче, adv., *to-day.*
ны́нѣ, adv., *to-day, now.*
ныть (за-ны́ть), *to ache*; но́ю,
но́ешь.
нѣ́житься, *to fondle itself.*
нѣ́когда, adv., *formerly.*
нѣмо́й, —а́я, —о́е, *dumb.*
нѣ́сколько, *some.*
нѣ́тъ, *not.*

о, interj., *o, oh !*
о (also объ and о́бо), prep.
with loc., *about.*
об-вива́ть (об-ви́ть), *to twine
round* (tr.).
об-жига́ть (об-же́чь), *to burn
up.*
оби́тель, —и, f., *monastery.*
о́блачко, *cloudlet.*
об-легча́ть (об-легчи́ть), *to
lighten.*
обма́нутый, *deceived.*
об-нима́ть (об-ня́ть and объ-
я́ть), *to embrace.*

об-о-жжённый, *burnt.*

óбразъ, *figure, form.*

об-рýшивать (об-рýшить), *to upset.*

объя́тіе, *embrace*; объя́тія (pl.), *arms.*

объя́тъ: pass. part. of объя́ть: see об-нима́ть.

обѣ́тъ, *a vow.*

огонёкъ, —нькá, *a little light.*

огóнь, огня́, m., *fire, light.*

о-дéжда, *dress.*

одинóкій, *solitary.*

одúпъ, однá, однó, *a*, *one, alone.*

однáжды, adv., *at one time, one day.*

о-заря́ть (о-зари́ть), *to illuminate.*

о-золоти́ться, *to turn golden.*

óко, —a, *eye*; pl. óчи, очéй.

о-крещáть (о-крести́ть), *to christen.*

о-кружённый, *surrounded.*

онъ, онá, онó, *he, she, it*; pl. они́, онѣ́, *they.*

опасáться (опасти́сь), *to dread.*

о-прáвленный, adj., *inlaid.*

о-про-ки́дываться (о-про-ки́нуться), *to turn upside down.*

опя́ть, adv., *again.*

орёлъ, орлá, *eagle.*

о-рýжіе, *weapon.*

о-свѣжáть (о-свѣжи́ть), *to refresh.*

осéнній, —яя,—ee, *autumnal.*

о-смáтриваться (о-смотрѣ́ться), *to look round, take one's bearings.*

о-ставáться (о-стáться), *to remain*; о-стаю́сь, о-стаёшься (о-стáнусь, о-стáнешься).

о-ставля́ть(о-стáвить),*to leave.*

о-стальнóй, —áя, —óe, *remaining.*

о-стáнься: imperative of о-стáться.

о-стáтокъ, —тка, *remnant, remains.*

óстровъ, *island*; pl. островá.

от-вергáть (от-вéргнуть), *to refuse.*

от-выкáть (от-вы́кнуть), *to become unaccustomed.*

от-вѣчáть (от-вѣ́тить), *to answer.*

отéцъ, отцá, *father.*

о-тирáть (о-терéть), *to wipe.*

от-кидáть(от-ки́нуть),*to throw back.*

от-ливáть (от-ли́ть), *to flow back.*

от-ливáться, *to glisten.*

от-ó-рванный: see от-рывáть.

от-пирáть (от-перéть), *to open.*

отрáдный, *consoling.*

от-рывáть (от-о-рвáть), *to tear off.*

от-тýда, adv., *from there.*

отцóвскій, *paternal.*

отчáяніе, *despair.*
отчáянный, *desperate.*
отчи́зна, *native country.*
отъ, prep. with gen., *from.*
о-цѣпенѣніе, *lethargy.*
очáгъ, —á, *hearth.*
óчи, очéй : pl. of óко.
очнýться, *to come back to one's senses.*

пáдать (у-пáсть), *to fall.*
пали́ть (вы́-палить), *to burn* (intr.).
пáмять, —и, f., *memory.*
пáра, *a pair.*
паръ, —а, *steam, vapour.*
пéрвый, *first.*
пéредъ, prep. with instr., *in front of, before.*
пере-носи́ть (пере-нести́), *to endure ; to transfer.*
песóкъ, —скá, *sand.*
пёстрый, *striped, speckled.*
пёсъ, пса, *a dog.*
печáлить (о-печáлить), *to distress.*
печáль, —и, f., *grief.*
печáльный, *sad.*
печáть, —и, f., *seal, impression.*
пи́ща, *food.*
плáкать (за-плáкать), *to weep, cry.*
плáменный, *fiery.*
плáмень, —я, m., *fire.*

пламенѣ́ть, *to flame, burn with rage.*
плескáть (плеснýть), *to splash.*
плитá, *a flagstone, flat stone.*
плóскій, *flat.*
плохóй, —áя, —óе, *bad.*
плы́ть (по-плы́ть), *to sail.*
плѣ́нный, adj., *captive.*
плѣнъ, —а, *captivity.*
плющъ, —á, *ivy.*
пля́ска, *a dance.*
по, prep. with acc., dat., or loc., *on, through, by, for.*
по-брёлъ : see брести́.
по-бѣждáть (по-бѣди́ть), *to conquer.*
по-вёртывать (по-вернýть), *to turn.*
пó-вѣсть, —и, f., *tale.*
по-вѣяла : see вѣять.
по-ги́бли : see ги́бнуть.
по-глощáть (по-глоти́ть), *to swallow up.*
по-гóня, *pursuit.*
по-гружённый, *plunged.*
под-зёмный, *subterranean.*
под-нимáть (под-ня́ть), *to raise.*
подóбаться, *to resemble.*
подóбіе, *a likeness.*
подóшва, *edge.*
подъ (and пóдо), prep. with instr. and acc., *under, to the sound of.*
поётъ : pres. tense of пѣть.

по-забывать (по-забыть), *to forget.*

поздній, —няя, —нее, *late.*

по-знавать(по-знать),*to know.*

по-зоръ, —а, *disgrace.*

по-искъ, *search.*

поить (на-поить), *to assuage.*

пока...не, *until.*

по-кидать(по-кинуть),*to leave behind.*

покой, —оя, *rest.*

по-кровъ, —а, *a pall, cover-let.*

по-крывать (по-крыть), *to cover.*

по-крытый, *covered.*

пол-день, полу-дня, m., *noon.*

пол-дневный, *of midday.*

поле, —я, *field.*

по-лётъ, —а, *flight.*

ползти (по-ползти), *to crawl, creep.*

полночный, adj., *midnight.*

полный, *full, plump.*

пологъ, *canopy.*

по-ложить : see класть.

полоса, *strip, band.*

полу-живой, *half-alive.*

польза, *use, advantage.*

поляна, *a clearing.*

по-мнить (вс-по-мнить), *to remember.*

по-мощь, —и, f., *help.*

по-нимать(по-нять),*to under-stand.*

пора, *time*; acc. пору; instr. порой, *at times.*

по-слышаться, *to resound.*

послѣ, adv., *afterwards.*

по-слѣдній, —яя, —ее, *last.*

по-стель, —и, f., *bed.*

по-стылый, *distasteful.*

по-текли : past tense of по-течь : see течь.

по-терять : see терять.

по-токъ, —а, *a torrent.*

по-тому, *therefore.*

по-томъ, adv., *afterwards, later.*

потъ, —а, *sweat.*

по-чему, *why.*

по-чуять : see чуять.

прахъ, —а, *dust.*

пре-воз-могать (пре-воз-мочь), *to get the better of.*

прѣдо = передъ.

пред-смертный, adj., *preced-ing death.*

пред-упреждать (пред-упре-дить), *to anticipate.*

предъ = передъ.

прежній, —няя, —нее, *for-mer.*

пре-красный, *beautiful.*

при, prep. with loc., *at, in, mid.*

при-вольный, *spacious.*

при-в-ставать (при-в-стать), *to rise a little.*

при-выкать (при-выкнуть),*to grow accustomed.*

при-вѣтливый, *friendly.*

при-вѣтъ, *greeting.*

при-жимáть (при-жáть), *to press.*

при-зирáть (прú-зрѣть), *to tend, protect.*

при-знавáть (при-знáть), *to confess, profess.*

прú-зрѣть: see при-зирáть.

при-зывáть (при-звáть), *to appeal to.*

при-легáть (при-лéчь), *to lie down.*

при-лéжный, *attentive.*

при-лéчь: see при-легáть.

при-мѣтно, adv., *noticeably.*

при-носúть (при-нестú), *to carry to.*

при-падáть (при-пáсть), *to fall upon.*

при-рóда, *Nature.*

при-ростáть (при-ростú), *to grow upon.*

при-слýшиваться (при-слýшаться), *to hearken.*

при-сылáть (при-слáть), *to send.*

при-ходúть (прі-йтú), *to approach.*

при-чýдливый, *fantastic.*

при-шёлъ: past tense of прі-йтú : see при-ходúть.

при-шлётъ: see при-сылáть.

прі-учáть (прі-учúть), *to habituate.*

прiютъ, *refuge.*

про, prep. with acc., *concerning.*

про-буждáться (про-будúться), *to awake.*

про-бѣгáть (про-бѣжáть), *to hurry past.*

про-должáться, *to continue.*

про-жигáть (про-жéчь), *to burn through.*

про-зрáчно, *transparently.*

про-зрáчный, *transparent.*

про-из-носúть(про-из-нестú), *to pronounce.*

про-йтú (про-ходúть), *to go forward, pass away.*

про-клинáть (про-клясть), *to curse.*

про-ложúть, *to set.*

про-мчáться, *to rush past.*

про-мѣнивать (про-мѣнять), *to exchange.*

прóпасть, —и, f., *pit, abyss.*

про-снýться: see про-сыпáться.

про-стёртый: past part. pass. of про-стерéть : see про-стирáть.

про-стирáть (про-стерéть), *to stretch out.*

простóй, *simple.*

про-сыпáться (про-снýться), *to wake up.*

протúвъ, prep. with gen., *opposite to.*

про-тяжный, *prolonged.*
про-хладный, *cool.*
про-ходить (про-йти), *to pass by.*
про-шедшее, *the past.*
про-шло : see про-ходить.
прошлый, adj., *past.*
прощай, *farewell* (imperative).
прощальный, *of farewell.*
прощеніе, *pardon.*
про-ѣзжать (про-ѣхать), *to travel through.*
прыгать (прыгнуть), *to bound, spring.*
прыжокъ, —жка, *a bound.*
прямой, —ая, —ое, *straight.*
прятать (с-прятать), *to hide.*
псовъ : gen. pl. of пёсъ.
птица, *bird.*
птичка, *little bird.*
пугать (ис-пугать), *to frighten.*
пугливый, *timid.*
пускай : imperative of пускать.
пускать (пустить), *to let.*
пускаться (пуститься), *to start.*
пустой, —ая, —ое, *empty.*
пустынный, *of the desert.*
пустыня, *a desert.*
путь, —и, m., *way, journey.*
пылающій, *flaming.*
пылкій, *fiery.*
пыль, —и, f., *dust.*
пышно, adv., *luxuriantly.*

пышный, *luxuriant.*
пѣнье, *singing.*
пѣсня, *a song.*
пѣть (с-пѣть), *to sing.*
пѣше-ходъ, *a foot-passenger.*

рабъ, —а, *slave.*
равный, *equal* ; всё равно, *it makes no difference.*
радужный, *of rainbow colours.*
радъ, рада, *glad.*
раждаться (родиться), *to be born.*
раз-валина, *a ruin.*
раз-веселять (раз-веселить), *to enliven.*
раз-вивать (раз-вить), *to develop.*
раз-говоръ, —а, *conversation*
раз-гонять (раз-о-гнать), *to disperse.*
раз-гульный, *disorderly.*
раз-даваться (раз-даться), *to spread, to be heard.*
раз-дѣлять (раз-дѣлить), *to separate.*
раз-личать (раз-личить), *to distinguish.*
разный, *different.*
раз-о-гнать : see раз-гонять.
разомъ, adv., *at the same time.*
раз-растать (раз-рости), *to grow up.*
раз-сказъ, —а, *a narrative.*

раз-ска́зывать (раз-сказа́ть), *to relate.*

раз-става́ться (раз-ста́ться), *to part.*

раз-сыпа́ть (раз-сы́пать), *to scatter.*

раз-сы́пчатый, *loose.*

раз-сѣка́ть (раз-сѣчь), *to cleave, split.*

разъ, —а, *time;* gen. pl. разъ; не разъ, *more than once.*

рай, ра́я, *heaven.*

ра́на, *a wound.*

рас-крыва́ть (рас-кры́ть), *to open.*

рас-пуска́ть (рас-пусти́ть), *to unfold.*

растѣ́ніе, *a plant.*

рвану́ться, *to charge.*

рвать (раз-о-рва́ть), *to tear.*

ребёнокъ, —нка, *a child;* pl. ребя́та.

ребя́ческій, *childish.*

ребя́чество, *childhood.*

ребя́чій, *childlike.*

ро́бкій, *timid.*

ро́вный, adj., *uniform.*

рога́тый, *forked.*

роди́мся : see рожда́ться.

роди́мый, *native.*

ро́дина, *native country.*

родно́й, —а́я, —о́е, *native.*

родны́е, —ы́хъ, noun, *relations.*

рождёнъ, —дена́,—дено́,*born.*

ро́за, *a rose.*

рой, ро́я, *a swarm.*

ро́потъ, *grumbling, complaint, murmur.*

роса́, *dew.*

Россі́я, —і́и, *Russia.*

ружьё, —ья́, n., *gun.*

рука́, *hand, arm.*

ру́сскій, *Russian.*

руче́й, —чья́, *a brook.*

ры́бка, *a fish.*

рыда́ть, *to sob.*

рыть (вы́-рыть), *to dig.*

рѣ́чка, *rivulet.*

рѣчь, —и, f., *a speech.*

сади́ться (сѣсть), *to sit down.*

садъ, —а, *garden.*

са́кля, *hut.*

самъ, сама́, само́, —*self;* plur. са́ми.

с-бива́ться(с-би́ться),*to stray.*

с-бра́сывать (с-бро́сить), *to throw off.*

сверка́ть (сверкну́ть), *to sparkle.*

с-вива́ться (с-ви́ться), *to twine* (intr.).

сводъ, —а, *a vault.*

свой, своя́, своё, *mine, thine, his.*

с-вы́ше, adv., *from on high.*

свѣ́жесть, —и, f., *freshness.*

свѣ́жій, *fresh.*

свѣти́ло, *star.*

свѣтлый, *bright.*

свѣтъ, —а, 1. *the world*; 2. *light.*

святой, —ая, —ое, *holy.*

священный, *sacred.*

с-гонять (со-гнать), *to banish.*

с-давливать(с-давить), *to compress.*

се, *lo !* (archaic).

себя, себѣ, собой, reflexive pron., *oneself, myself, thyself,* etc.

семейство, *family.*

сердито, adv., *angrily.*

сердитый, *angry.*

сердце, *heart.*

серебрястый, *silvery.*

серебро, *silver.*

серна, *a chamois.*

серьга, *ear-ring*; pl. серьги.

сестра, *sister*; pl. сёстры, сестёръ.

с-жигать (с-жечь), *to burn* (tr.).

с-жимать (с-жать), *to compress.*

с-зывать (со-звать), *to summon.*

сидѣть (по-сидѣть), *to be sitting.*

сила, *strength.*

силиться, *to force oneself.*

сильно, comp. —нѣй, adv., *powerfully.*

сильный, *powerful.*

синева, *blueness.*

сирота, *an orphan.*

сіяніе, *glitter.*

сіять (за-сіять), *to shine.*

скажи: imperative of сказать: see говорить.

сказать: see говорить.

скала, *cliff.*

скачокъ, —чка, *a spring.*

скважина, *a crack.*

сквозь,prep. with acc., *through.*

с-клоняться (с-клониться), *to stoop.*

скользить (скользнуть), *to slip, slide.*

скоро, adv., *quickly.*

скорый, *quick.*

с-крывать (с-крыть), *to hide.*

слабый, *weak.*

слава, *glory.*

сладкій, *sweet.*

сладко, adv., *sweetly.*

сладостный, *sweet, soft.*

сладостнѣй, *more sweetly.*

сладость, —и, f., *sweetness.*

слеза, *a tear*; n. pl. слёзы.

с-ливаться (с-литься), *to flow together, mingle.*

слово, *a word.*

слушать (по-слушать), *to listen.*

слышать (у-слышать), *to hear.*

слышный, *audible.*

слѣдить (по-слѣдить), *to follow* (*with the eyes*).

слѣдовать (по-слѣдовать), *to follow*; impers. слѣдуетъ, *it is proper.*

слѣдъ, —á, *a trace, footprint.*

смертéльный, *deadly.*

смерть, —и, f., *death.*

с-метáть (с-местú), *to brush off.*

с-молкáть (с-мóлкнуть), *to be silent.*

смотрѣть (по-смотрѣть), *to look.*

смýглый, *sunburnt, swarthy.*

смýтно, adv., *dimly.*

смýтный, *dim, confused.*

смущáть (смутúть), *to confuse.*

с-мыкáть (со-мкнýть), *to shut up.*

смѣть (по-смѣть), *to dare.*

смѣяться (за-смѣяться), *to laugh.*

с-началá, adv., *at first.*

с-нóва, adv., *again.*

сновъ : gen. pl. of сонъ.

сномъ : instr. of сонъ.

снѣ : loc. of сонъ.

снѣговóй, —áя, —óe, *snowy.*

снѣгъ, —a, *snow*; pl. снѣгá.

со = съ.

со-бирáть (со-брáть), *to collect.*

со-жглá: past tense of с-жечь: see жечь.

со-зовý : see с-зывáть.

со-йтúться : see с-ходúться.

сóлнце, *sun.*

со-мкнýть : see с-мыкáть.

со-мнѣніе, *doubt.*

сонный, *sleeping.*

сонъ, сна, *a dream, sleep.*

со-рвáвшись : see с-рывáть.

со-сѣдство, *neighbourhood.*

сóтня, —и, *a hundred.*

со-шлá : past tense of со-йтú : see с-ходúть.

спасáть (спастú), *to save.*

спать (по-спáть), *to sleep*; сплю, спишь, etc. ; past tense спалъ, спалá.

спинá, *back.*

с-плетáть (с-плестú), *to coil up* (intr.).

спóрить (по-спóрить), *to contend.*

споръ, —a, *contention, dispute.*

с-пускáться (с-пустúться), *to descend.*

с-пýтанный, *mixed up.*

средь, prep. with gen., *amid.*

с-рывáть (со-рвáть), *to tear away.*

стáдо, *a flock.*

становúться (стать), *to become.*

стáну : pres. of стать.

старúкъ, —á, *old man.*

стáрость, —и, f., *old age.*

стать, *to become, begin*; стáну, —ешь ; past tense сталъ.

степно́й, —а́я, —о́е, adj., *of the steppes.*

степь, —и, f., *steppe, prairie.*

с-тиха́ть(с-ти́хнуть), *to be still.*

столбъ, —а́, *a pillar.*

с-толпля́ться (с-толпи́ться), *to crowd together.*

сто́лько, *so many.*

стона́ть (за-стона́ть), *to moan.*

стонъ, —а, *a groan.*

сторона́, *side, country.*

страда́ніе, *suffering.*

страда́ть (по-страда́ть), *to suffer.*

стражъ, *a guardian.*

страна́, *country.*

стра́нный, *strange.*

страсть, —и, f., *passion.*

страхъ, —а, *fear.*

страши́ть, *to frighten.*

стра́шно, adv., *terribly.*

стра́шный, *terrible.*

страшнѣ́й, *more terrible.*

стрекоза́, *dragon-fly.*

стро́йнный, *shapely.*

струи́ться, *to flow, stream.*

струя́, *stream.*

ступе́нь, —и, f., *a step.*

стыдъ, —а́, *shame.*

стѣна́, *a wall.*

судьба́, *fortune.*

сукъ, —а́, *a bough;* pl. су́чья.

су́мракъ, *dusk.*

су́мрачный, *gloomy.*

сухо́й, —а́я, —о́е, *dry.*

с-хва́тывать (с-хвати́ть), *to catch up.*

с-ходи́ть (со-йти́), *to descend.*

с-ходи́ться (со-йти́ться), *to come together.*

съ or со, prep. with gen., *from.*

съ or со, prep. with instr., *with.*

сыро́й, —а́я, —о́е, *damp, raw.*

сѣдо́й, —а́я, —о́е, *grey-haired.*

сѣдо́къ, —а́, *rider.*

сѣлъ: see сади́ться.

сюда́, adv., *hither.*

табу́нъ, —а́, *drove of horses.*

таи́нственный, *mysterious.*

таи́ть (у-таи́ть), *to conceal.*

та́йна, *a secret.*

та́йный, *secret.*

та́к-же, *also.*

тако́въ, —ва́, —во́, *such.*

тако́й, —а́я, —о́е, *such;* тако́й-то, *such-and-such.*

такъ, adv., *thus, as follows.*

тамъ, adv., *there.*

тебѣ́: dat. of ты.

тебя́: acc. and gen. of ты.

темни́чный, *of a prison.*

темнота́, *darkness.*

тёмный, *dark.*

тепе́рь, adv., *now.*

терно́вникъ, *thorn-bush.*

терно́вый, adj., *of thorns.*

терпѣ́ть (по-терпѣ́ть), *to endure.*

теря́ть (по-теря́ть), *to lose.*

течь (по-тéчь), *to flow.*
Тифлúсъ, —а, *Tiflis.*
тúхій, *still, quiet.*
тúхо, *quietly, slowly.*
тихóнько, *very slowly.*
тúше, adv., *more slowly.*
тишинá, *silence.*
тлѣ́ть, *to moulder.*
тó ... тó, *at one time ... at another.*
тогдá, adv., *then.*
той : gen. sing. fem. of тотъ.
толпá, *a crowd.*
тóлько, adv., *only.*
томúться (ис - томúться), *to grow weary.*
томý : dat. of тотъ.
томъ : loc. of тотъ.
тонýть (у-тонýть), *to float.*
тóполь, —я, m., *poplar.*
топóрѣ, —á, *axe.*
торжéственный, *solemn, triumphant.*
торжествовáть, *to triumph.*
тоскá, *painful longing, misery.*
тотчáсъ, adv., *at once.*
тотъ, та, то, demonstr. pron., *that.*
тотъ же, *the same.*
травá, *grass.*
трáтить(по-трáтить), *to spend.*
тревóга, *excitement.*
трель, —и, f., *hum.*
трепетáть (за-трепетáть), *to flicker.*

трéпетъ, *tremor.*
трёхъ: gen. of три.
три, *three.*
трóгать (трóнуть), *to touch, move.*
тройнóй, *triple.*
тропá, *a path.*
тростнúкъ, —á, *a reed.*
трýдный, *toilsome.*
трудъ, —á, *toil, difficulty.*
трупъ, —á, *dead body.*
тудá, adv., *thither.*
тумáнный, *misty, lack-lustre.*
тумáнъ, —а, *mist.*
тутъ, adv., *there.*
тýча, *a cloud.*
тýчка, *little cloud.*
тщéтно, adv., *vainly.*
ты, *thou* ; pl. вы.
тьма, *darkness.*
тѣ : plur. of тотъ.
тѣ́ло, *body.*
тѣмъ : instr. of тотъ.
тѣнь, —и, f., *shadow, tinge.*
тѣснúться, *to press close.*
тѣхъ : gen. pl. of тотъ.
тюрьмá, *prison.*
тяжёлый, *heavy.*
тянýть (по-тянýть), *to stretch.*
тянýться (по - тянýться), *to stretch* (intr.).

у, prep. with gen., *in the case of, belonging to.*

у-бѣгáть (у-бѣжáть), *to run away.*

увы́, *alas.*

у-вѣренный, *convinced.*

у-вѣщевáніе, *exhortation.*

у-гáдывать (у-гадáть), *to guess.*

у-гасáть (у-гáснуть), *to be extinguished.*

угловóй, —áя, —óе, adj., *corner.*

угрю́мый, *sullen.*

удалéцъ, —льцá, *hero.*

удáръ, —a, *a blow.*

ударять (удáрить), *to strike.*

у-дручáть (у-дручи́ть), *to weigh down.*

ужáсный, *terrible.*

ужé (and ужъ), adv., *already ;* ужé не or не ужъ, *no longer.*

у́зкій, *narrow.*

у-знавáть (у-знáть), *to learn.*

узóръ, —a, *pattern, tracery.*

укóръ, —a, *reproach.*

у-мирáть (у-мерéть), *to die.*

у-мру́ : pres. tense of у-мерéть.

умъ, —á, *reason, the mind.*

у-носи́ть (у-нести́ or у-нéсть), *to carry away.*

у-пáлъ : see пáдать.

у-пивáться (у-пи́ться), *to intoxicate oneself.*

у-прямый, *obstinate.*

у-си́ливать (у-си́лить), *to strengthen.*

у-сни́ : imperative of у-снýть : see у-сыпáть.

у-спѣвáть (у-спѣть), *to have time.*

устá, устъ, pl. n., *lips.*

у-ставáть (у-стáть), *to grow weary.*

у-стáлый, *weary.*

у-стремлять (у-стреми́ть), *to direct.*

у-ступáть (у-ступи́ть), *to yield.*

у-сыпáть (у-снýть), *to go to sleep.*

у-таю : see тáйть.

у-тихáть (у-ти́хнуть), *to calm down.*

у́тренній, *of morning.*

у́тро, *morning.*

у-тѣха, *amusement.*

у-ходи́ть (у-йти́), *to go away.*

ущéлье, *a gorge.*

хвалéніе, *praise.*

хвостъ, —á, *tail.*

хлáдный = холóдный.

холмъ, —á, *a hill.*

холóдный, *cold.*

хóлодъ, noun, *cold.*

хоровóдъ, *a company.*

хотѣть (за-хотѣть), *to wish.*

хотя́ (and хоть), *although, at least ;* хотя́ бы, *if only.*

храни́тельный, *protecting.*

храни́ть (со-храни́ть), *to preserve.*

хребе́тъ, —бта́, *ridge.*
хруста́ль, —я́, f., *clearness.*
худо́й, —а́я, —6е, *thin.*

ца́рство, *kingdom.*
царь, —я́, *king, ruler.*
цвѣсти́ (за-цвѣсти́), *to flourish.*
цвѣто́къ, —тка́, *a flower.*
цвѣтъ, —a, *a flower.*
церко́вный, *of the church.*
цѣль, —и, f., *aim.*
цѣпь, —и, f., *a chain.*

чадра́, *a robe.*
часъ, —a, *hour.*
ча́ща, —и, *jungle.*
чей, чья, чьё, adj., *whose;* ни
    чей, *belonging to no one.*
чело́, *forehead.*
человѣкъ, —a, *a man.*
червь, —я́, m., *a worm.*
череда́, *turn, order.*
чернёцъ, —еца́, *a monk.*
чёрный, *black.*
чернѣть, *to be black.*
чета́, *a pair.*
чешуя́, *scales.*
чи́стый, *pure, clean.*
что, *that, what.*
чтó-бы (and чтобъ), *that, in*
    order to.
чу́вство, *feeling.*
чу́вствовать(по-чу́вствовать),
    to feel.
чу́дный, *wonderful.*

чу́ждый, *foreign.*
чужо́й, —а́я, —6е, *foreign.*
чу́ять (по-чу́ять), *to scent.*

шага́ть (шагну́ть), *to step.*
шагъ, —a, *a step;* pl. шаги́.
шака́лъ, *a jackal.*
шевели́ть(шевельну́ть),*to stir.*
шелести́ть, *to rustle.*
шепта́ть(шепну́ть),*to whisper.*
шерсть, —и, f., *fur.*
шесть, —и́, *six.*
широ́кій, *broad.*
шла, *(she) walked;* fem. past
    tense of идти́.
шо́рохъ, *rustling.*
штыкъ, —а́, *a bayonet.*
шу́мный, *noisy.*
шумъ, —a, *noise.*
шумѣть (за-шумѣть), *to make*
    a noise.

щека́, *cheek;* pl. щёки.

э́тотъ, э́та, э́то, *this.*

ю́ность, —и, f., *youth.*
ю́ный, *young.*

я, меня́, мнѣ, мно́ю or мной,
    I, me, etc.
явля́ться (яви́ться), *to appear.*
язы́къ, —а́, *tongue, language.*
я́ркій, *bright.*
я́сный, *clear.*
яснѣ́й, adv., *clearer, more clear.*

For EU product safety concerns, contact us at Calle de José Abascal, 56–1°,
28003 Madrid, Spain or eugpsr@cambridge.org.

www.ingramcontent.com/pod-product-compliance
Ingram Content Group UK Ltd.
Pitfield, Milton Keynes, MK11 3LW, UK
UKHW012333130625
459647UK00009B/258